The Strikebreakers

The Report of the Strikebreaking
Committee of the Ontario Federation of
Labour and the Labour Council of
Metropolitan Toronto

*Written by Marc Zwelling
for the Ontario Federation of
Labour and the Labour Council of
Metropolitan Toronto*

TORONTO
1972

ISBN 0-88770-179-5

Distributed by *new press*
Order Department
553 Richmond Street West
Toronto 133, Ontario

Manufactured in Canada

 37

Contents

Introduction

Strikebreaking became a public issue throughout Ontario in 1971, with the discovery of wiretapping devices at the strike headquarters of unions and the presence of well-organized professional strikebreaking crews at many picket lines. Expressing their concern, which reflected that of the Legislature and the public at large, the delegates to the November, 1971 convention of the Ontario Federation of Labour endorsed strong resolutions calling for action against professional strikebreakers and protection from wiretappers.

In late 1971, acting on their convention mandate, officers of the Federation and representatives of the Labour Council of Metropolitan Toronto explored the feasibility of a joint and wide-ranging investigation into these anti-labour practices. The purpose of the investigation was to discover all that could be known about the operations, motives, connections and effects of strikebreakers and other agents of union destruction. The goal of the joint committee of Labour Council and O.F.L. representatives was to put into the hands of unionists and the public as well the important facts about activities that appeared to threaten the balance of collective bargaining power and the security of the community itself wherever professional strikebreakers were employed.

Strikebreaking is of concern at this moment to the Legislature of the province. The Minister of Labour, Fernand Guindon, has said, "Personally, I don't like the idea of professional strikebreakers. . . ." His deputy minister, Robert Johnston, told a legislative committee in June that professional strikebreakers are "certainly not making life any easier for us. . . ." Guindon said he would consider legislation to deal with the problem, "But I would certainly think that we have to get all the information first to make sure we're coming up with the right legislation, if necessary."

The Labour Minister underscored the danger of professional strikebreakers to a society organized on order and law and to an economic system that benefits from stable industrial relations. Strikebreaking, Guindon observed in 1972, "does create hard feelings". He added, "Our people, our mediators have to pick up all the pieces . . . and try to get a settlement."

Industrial relations with industrial peace is the goal of labour legislation of the province. The preamble to the Labour Relations Act declares collective bargaining between unions and employers "is in the public interest of the Province of Ontario. . . ." Major government task forces, royal commissions and special inquiries prepared the Woods Report, the Rand Report and the Little Report to help governments make policies on labour-management relations.

Time and time again the courts have supplemented the law and supported the right to collective bargaining and the right to organization of employees. Governments have recognized that labour relations are not merely the affairs of unions and employers, however. The public's interest is at stake in the outcome of free collective bargaining. Attempts to subvert that process are threats to the well-being and security of the population as a whole. A judge in the United States crystallized the impact of bargaining and when necessary striking when he said, "The health of the present generation and of those yet unborn may depend on these matters, and the practices in a single factory may have economic repercussions upon a whole region and affect widespread systems of marketing."[*]

The investigation that produced these findings concludes that at some time, strikers, management, the police and the government are all potential victims of professional strikebreakers. It is incumbent on all of them to know everything they can before making the decisions that affect the lives of many people.

The findings in this book are the result of research and investigation conducted in the first six months of 1972. Some material collected previously has been re-checked to authenticate it. The vast majority of the information comes from the mouths of strikebreakers, industrial spies, their agents and contacts. Where published material and public records have been used, these sources are cited in footnotes.

The Ontario Federation of Labour financed much of the investigation. The original concept and a great deal of assistance necessary to complete the research were the contributions of the Labour Council of Metropolitan Toronto. Many sources in unions and managements contributed what facts they knew. The help of all who were important to the investigation cannot be acknowledged. Some, for their protection, must remain confidential.

An investigation—even of this scope in terms of time and resources—can barely open a crack in the wall of mystery that

*Thornhill v. Alabama, 310 U.S. (1940).

shields professional strikebreaking rackets and labour-spy rings operating in Ontario today. Although the sponsors obviously are committed to eradicating these and other anti-union practices, everything possible was done to conduct the investigation in a dispassionate and comprehensive manner. What follows are the facts that can be discerned with the limited resources of private citizens. Only the government has the capacity to conduct a definitive investigation.

Ultimately, the choice whether to accommodate professional strikebreakers and anti-union spies and mercenaries and compromise civil liberties and freedoms is the decision of society as a whole. This report makes clear that professional strikebreaking is a volatile practice. If government does not expurgate it, unhappy consequences are sure to result.

The help of those involved in preparing this report should be cited. Laurel MacDowell and Cathy Dean worked on the research. The effort of the manuscript typist, who modestly wishes no credit, is gratefully appreciated.

Finally, this report is dedicated to people who, regardless of whether they have personal commitment in unions or managements, love peace and freedom and are willing to defend those precious rights.

Marc Zwelling
July, 1972
Toronto

1

One of the World's Oldest Professions

The right of labour to organize into unions without interference, coercion, and intimidation derives from the exercise
of the rights of free speech, peaceable assembly, and freedom
of the press. . . .[1]

Canada occupies a unique place in the world of nations. It is
the only country of importance where there are no restrictions
on the intervention for profit of private, third parties in labour-
management relations. Nowhere else in the world is professional
strikebreaking tolerated but in Canada.

Even in the United States of America, where the professional
strikebreaking racket began and flourished to a multi-million-
dollar business,[2] it has now almost vanished. In 40 states[3] there
are controls of some kind on professional strikebreakers and
anti-union spies. But anti-labour rackets operate openly and
lucratively in Canada.

There are many ways to break a strike. The most common is
replacing the strikers. Convincing the strikers to desert their
picket line and return to work without a union or a contract—
on the employer's terms—is another way.

With replacements taking over the strikers' jobs, the shipment
of products from the plant is the *coup de grace* in the successful
strikebreaking operation.

It was not always so simple. In the United States, the birth-
place of professional strikebreaking, violence was often a tactic
of the strikebreaking agencies. Public outrage over the strikebreaking rackets led to a major investigation of the business
beginning in 1936, when the Senate Committee on Education

and Labour probed the underworld of labour spies and union-busters.

The purpose of the committee, headed by Senator Robert M. La Follette Jr., was "to investigate violation of the right of free speech and assembly and interference with the right of labour to organize and bargain collectively".

Even before the La Follette disclosures, the American people had seen the violence engendered by strikebreaking. In 1892 Andrew Carnegie's steel company in Homestead, Pennsylvania, near Pittsburgh, hired a 300-man army from William and Robert Pinkerton to break a strike of 3,800 workers. The results were 118 casualties, including 35 dead. What had begun as a lockout ended as "one of the most murderous and dramatic tragedies in U.S. labour-management annals".[4] Carnegie's mill remained non-union until 44 years later.

During a 1913-1914 miners' strike at John D. Rockefeller Jr.'s Colorado Fuel and Iron Company, 13 women and children and six strikers were gunned down by private company guards and the militia in Ludlow, Colorado.

The history of the United States is blotched with bloody episodes like Homestead and Ludlow. In every case, the presence of strikebreakers provoked violence. In 1907, during a San Francisco street-car strike, a dozen men were killed, and 52 were hurt. That was the last strike invaded by Jim Farley, a well-known recruiter of anti-union labour.[5]

Farley's successor was Pearl L. Bergoff, a flamboyant Easterner who advertised 172 strikes handled. A journalist of the 1930's compiled the morbid record of fatalities sustained by both sides in Bergoff strikes, and it totalled:

Strikers killed by strikebreakers	17
Strikebreakers killed by strikers	6
Men, women and children killed by strikebreaker-driven trolley cars	21
Bystander killed by strikebreakers	1
Strikebreakers killed at work (two of them on trolleys)	3
Strikebreakers killed by strikebreakers in barracks	4
Strikebreakers killed in Bergoff's New York Office	2
Total killed	54[6]

The Canadian story is more difficult to assemble. Labour historian Stuart Jamieson, who surveyed industrial unrest for the 1968 federal government Task Force on Labour Relations, believes there has been "a sort of 'conspiracy of silence' about the whole subject of labour unrest and industrial conflict, particularly of the more violent kind, in this country".[7] He blames historians' "mistaken or misguided image" of the Canadian people for the omission. In every violent strike Jamieson was able to document, however, strikebreakers appear in each, doubtlessly as the catalyst for disorder.

In a 1906 sawmill strike in Buckingham, Quebec, private security guards were brought in to protect strikebreakers. Two strikers were shot and killed, several others were hurt. One "detective" also was killed.[8]

Three years earlier an organizer for the United Brotherhood of Railway Employees, Frank Rogers, was gunned down while picketing the Canadian Pacific Railway yards in Vancouver. His murderers were "a gang of thugs" employed by the company.[9]

Jamieson intimates that if records were more complete, history might show that Canadian employers were more than ready to use any means possible to resist unions.

"Employers in Canada," he says, "are and have been no less hostile to unions than were their American counterparts. Indeed, the record seems to indicate that they were even more hostile in some respects."

They had help, of course. Violence, sometimes official violence, has been almost common. In 1918, a British Columbia coal miners' organizer, Albert (Ginger) Goodwin, was slain by an unidentified assassin, alleged to be a provincial policeman.[10] In 1929, Viljo Rosval and John Voutilainen disappeared after leaving a lumberworkers' camp that was on strike near Port Arthur, Ontario, in the small town of Onion Lake. Later that winter, in 1930, the bodies of the two unionists were found in a small creek. The coroner said it was drowning—in three feet of water.[11]

In 1931 in Estevan, Saskatchewan, three picketing coal miners were shot and killed by a young Royal Canadian Mounted Police constable.[12]

In 1963, three striking members of the Lumber and Sawmill Workers' Union were shot and killed, and nine others were wounded, in a clash with strikebreakers near Kapuskasing, Ontario, at Reesor Siding.[13]

The 19 strikebreakers charged initially with non-capital murder were acquitted. They paid fines of $100 apiece for possession of offensive weapons. Two hundred strikers were fined a total of $27,600 for unlawful assembly.

What was remarkable about the incident at Reesor Siding was that it happened after continual warnings to the provincial government of Premier John Robarts that violence was likely. ". . . Had anyone listened to the voices of the people of the north," said MPP Vernon Singer four days after the shootings, "to the mayor of Kapuskasing, who said weeks ago that there would be violence and danger, then proper steps would have to be taken, could have been taken, and should have been taken to prevent this tragedy having happened in this province."[14]

The La Follette hearing in the United States also focused on anti-union espionage. Some of the practices had been divulged by the muckrakers, but La Follette's disclosures were even grislier. La Follette disclosed that spying "was a common, if not the universal, practice in American industry".[15] The purpose was to prevent unions from getting into plants and offices. Companies of all sizes used spies, the committee learned. "No firm is too small to employ them."[16]

Some spies instigated acts of sabotage to discredit the union or to engineer dismissal of union sympathizers. The La Follette transcripts tell of a spy in 1936 in Kent, Ohio, who urged his fellow employees to dynamite a struck plant. The Burns Detective Agency, Pinkerton's Detective Agency and other private investigation concerns supplied the spies. The bill for spying in a four-year period was nearly $10 million, the La Follette investigators learned. A contemporary of La Follette's, writing in a law journal, explained why spies were important in anti-union strategies.

It is ever true that the employer has everything to gain by encouraging violence after a strike has begun, since the result is always likely to be direct suppression of the striking element by the forces of organized government, or at the very least, the marshalling of public opinion against the strikers. On the other hand, the strikers have everything to lose by rioting and fighting, and in fact the union leaders usually go out of their way to avoid any violent display or destruction of property.[17]

American observers of the industrial-relations scene agree that now that industrial espionage (the kind directed against unions, anyway) has been made illegal, its use has declined.

What stands out about the La Follette disclosures even today, 35 years and more after their release, is how pertinent the committee's findings are to the climate of labour relations in Ontario in 1972.

The committee's conclusions about the use of private security guards in strikes could be transplanted to Ontario at this moment. For example, the committee found that the presence of strikeguards "far from providing order or protection, usually resulted in disorder and violence". The role of most guards in strike situations "appears to be the deliberate exercise of intimidation and terror".

Further, the committee concluded that strikebreakers and strikeguards were "the implements of a labour policy based on the rejection of collective bargaining".

And furthermore, "Professional strikeguards and strikebreakers are worse than useless in preventing acts of lawlessness or violence by strikers. Instead of controlling or pacifying such situations, they embitter them and add further fuel to the flames."

The private guards and professional strikebreakers, La Follette's committee declared, have a conflict of interest in a labour-management dispute since they have "a pecuniary incentive to create and maintain a state of disorder. . . ."

Why has the old profession of strikebreaking, on the continent since the 1880's, enjoyed such longevity? Generally, it is the prerogative of the government in power to halt strikebreaking. If anti-union espionage and strikebusting are condoned, then it must be said public opinion demands that they be condoned.

The education system and the mass media can be blamed for the prevalent anti-labour feeling expressed in official sanction for strikebreaking. A recent study by researchers at the Ontario Institute for Studies in Education, in Toronto, found the treatment that the labour movement gets in the school textbooks our children read is "all too often perfunctory, imperceptive, and inaccurate".[18] The textbooks "tend to emphasize violence" and imply "that all the violence emanated from one side. . . ."[19]

The mass media, too, are responsible for anti-labour attitudes. Public opinion polls confirm that not only is the image of organized labour low, it is sinking all the time.[20] Even a Tory party Labour Minister, Dalton Bales, has remarked that because the media concentrate on strikes in labour reporting, "an impression of almost constant labour-management turmoil is created".[21]

Hysteria is the most apt way of describing the coverage of most labour affairs in the mass media. An example cited to the federal government's Task Force on Labour Relations shows how a typical major labour news story is presented. During the week-long national railway strike in 1950, it was reported by "a reputable newsman" that there were "around 500,000 Canadians idle as a direct result of the strike". If the strike were not ended soon, the report said, "this figure will soar to 750,000". The actual number of striking or laid off railway workers was 199,000, the number laid off in other industries because of it, 23,000.[22]

Many American labour experts conclude surveys of public-interest disputes and laws to curb "emergency" strikes with implicit criticism of the media. "Although we do not know as much as we would like about the impact of utility strikes," goes a typical observation, "there are good and sufficient reasons for believing their effects have been exaggerated."[23]

Even hospital strikes and massive transportation strikes do not qualify as emergencies to detached observers, since they do not (or have not yet) put an intolerable burden on a community or country. Inconvenience is a more likely result than hardship.

Even intellectuals are not immune to anti-union attitudes, although they at least should be able to keep an open mind. One explanation given recently is that the well-educated are overly sentimental about rank-and-file unionists. Small-l liberals who vilify labour leaders are "unable to champion the cause of the poor and the disadvantaged without idealizing them as well. As a result . . . these critics could seldom bring themselves to blame union shortcomings on the members; instead, they conclude that the leaders must somehow be responsible."[24]

A great amount of criticism about unions ought to be ignored, because each group in the best position to influence public opinion (the powerful, the wealthy and their mouthpieces, the mass media) "has its special reason for misconceiving the role of the union leader and exaggerating his influence".[25]

Businessmen are obviously inclined to blame their problems on "some opportunistic union leader who has succeeded in leading the workers astray". It would be "most disagreeable to concede that wages are kept unfairly low or that the quest for efficiency had led to harsh supervision or uncomfortable working conditions".[26]

Unions themselves respond languidly to the anti-labour feelings swelling around them. Organized labour, as the public relations director of the Quebec Federation of Labour said in 1969, is "too often a prisoner and a victim of its own propaganda". There is no labour press of any consequence in the country to retaliate against the attacks of the establishment media.

The unions are unable to correct their own tarnished image, and the educational system and the mass media are unwilling to do so. Only government is left to displace fantasy with truth in labour-management relations. But government too seems hardly willing. In all the publications of the Ontario Labour Department, not one tells how to form a union. Of course government officials argue it is not their job as supposedly neutral third parties in labour relations to instruct workers on organizing themselves. Then is it the job of the government to publish regularly the statistics on strikes and wage settlements that are used as propaganda against the unions? The federal labour department used to report the outcome of strikes. From 1900 to 1930, 1,361 work stoppages were settled in favour of employers, according to the federal survey, but only 1,072 in favour of employees. The department has stopped keeping such statistics.[27]

There are no national statistics available in Canada on the number of industrial injuries and illnesses, or on the working days lost by disabling maladies suffered in the plants and shops of Canadian businessmen. But individual provincial workmen's compensation board reports indicate the time lost to injuries and sickness is consistently 10 times the days lost annually to strikes.

The federal task force's labour historian reported that "strikes and lockouts result from only a small fraction, generally less than five per cent, of collective bargaining negotiations and involve a correspondingly small percentage of workers bound by union agreements. Only rarely do strikes account for as much as one-half of one per cent of total man-days of employment over the nation as a whole during any given year."[28]

In comparison with the restraints on organized labour in this country, business is treated lightly by government regulation. Says one economist, ". . . There are few effective restrictions on the activities of large corporations, and they do not have to give an account of their activities to anyone."[29]

It's incongruous that a public that supports more stringent laws against unions and strikes should be so ill-served by its governments.

In Sweden, by contrast, "union organization and collective bargaining became accepted as legitimate and positive forces in the industrial economy at an early date," says an industrial-relations specialist. "This . . . is in strong contrast to developments in Canada. . . ."[30]

What Canadians have in return for their anti-union attitudes and their strict labour legislation is not less industrial strife than Sweden and the United States, but more.

Significantly, the time lost due to strikes or lockouts as a percentage of all non-agricultural working time has declined dramatically in this century to almost zero in Sweden, where more than 84 per cent of the workers are in unions. But in the United States (28.4 per cent organized) the amount of time lost has remained the same. In Canada, where less than one-third of the workers are organized, the time lost has actually increased.[31]

Collective bargaining, and the right to organize without fear of dismissal for union activity, were guaranteed in Sweden in 1906 by an agreement between big federations of unions and management. Not until 1944 did workers in Canada get the right in legislation to organize and bargain collectively, 12 years after American labour won those same principles in law.[32] Unions are so accepted in Sweden that even with the closed shop almost non-existent the potential work force that can be organized is considered "saturated". Compulsory arbitration "has never gained a foothold."[33] What one writer calls "the remarkably peaceful conditions . . . prevalent in the Swedish labour market" are the result of "the employers' understanding of the importance of having a strong trade union movement as their counterpart".[34]

If there is a link between strikebreaking, the public's tolerance of anti-labour attitudes, and government acquiescence to public prejudice, then the judicial system is also responsible.

The intervention of legal authorities and the courts in labour-management matters has served to suppress real public debate on working conditions and economic power. The subterfuge of legality cloaks industrial relations in moral questions. As Jamieson notes, "Where violence did develop in the course of labour disputes, police or military forces were used in the overwhelming majority of cases to protect employers' property and freedom of action to recruit strikebreakers, rather than to protect strikers' rights to safeguard their jobs."[35]

That has generally been true of the role of the law in labour relations in North America. There are a few, certainly rare, exceptions. In 1934, Milwaukee city fathers jailed 150 of the Pearl Bergoff gang when they attempted to break a strike of operators for the city's privately-owned street railway company. It was a turnabout for America's No. 1 strikebreaker, because "a duly constituted government not only sanctioned Pearl Bergoff's start as a professional strikebreaker but helped provide the means for it".[36] New York City actually gave Bergoff his first business, $24,054 to break a garbagemen's strike in 1907.

But in a 1934 cotton-mill strike at Bibb Manufacturing Company, in Georgia, Governor Eugene Talmadge ordered Bergoff men chased from the state. "It is not clear," said one observer, "whether Governor Talmadge stopped the strikebreaking or merely superseded the strikebreakers."[37]
But,

. . . the attempts of governors, mayors, and chiefs of police to prevent, by executive action, violence and destruction at the hands of imported gangsters have been, if possible, even more ineffectual than legislative action. For efforts to keep out or arrest strikebreakers have uniformly been blocked through the issuance of injunctions by courts to whom the nebulous and once sacrosanct property right—to conduct one's business as one sees fit—still seems important enough to demand protection even at a sacrifice of the public peace and order.[38]

In Canada the story has been the same, though no records exist to show any public official ever restraining the use of strikebreakers.[39]

The presence of the R.C.M.P. throughout Canadian history, says Stuart Jamieson, "has been felt with enough force to tip the scales of battle in hundreds of strikes and labour demonstrations".[40]

Canadian judges and public officials have hid behind law-and-order arguments to conceal union-busting by public authorities, although few probably have ever gone as far in their public or private statements as William Howard Taft, then a judge, later a U.S. president, who wrote to his wife during a bloody railway strike in 1894: "It will be necessary for the military to kill some of the mob before the trouble can be stayed. They have only killed six . . . as yet. This is hardly enough to make an impression".[41]

When up to 400 Ontario Provincial Police marched into Kirkland Lake during a 1942 miners' strike, when 100 Quebec Provincial Police invaded the town of Asbestos to protect hundreds of strikebreakers in the 1949 asbestos-workers' strike, and when 300 O.P.P constables arrived in Sudbury during the 1966 strike at International Nickel Company of Canada, Canadian authorities were repeating a history of official sanction of the use of force in labour disputes in North America.

Speaking of the early years of turmoil, Jamieson observes, "Little wonder, then, that this era of industrial unrest left a long legacy of distrust of and hostility to governments and a contempt for the law among many in the ranks of organized labour. It was a legacy that was to generate recurrent trouble on a large scale in subsequent decades."[42]

The official sanction government and judiciary give to strike-breaking dates back to the original sin of unions: they were construed as conspiracies. From 1806 to 1842, there were 17 trials in the United States in which unions were charged with engaging in criminal conspiracy. In anti-conspiracy demonstrations in New York City and Washington, D.C., two judges were burned in effigy. In the landmark court case of *Commonwealth v. Hunt*, in 1842, a judge overturned a lower court ruling that unions were unlawful conspiracies. That unions "may have a tendency to impoverish another, that is, to diminish his gains and profits", does not constitute illegal activity, the court ruled.[43]

The case was instrumental in changing attitudes, but it did not prevent more anti-union harassment by the courts.

There were actually more conspiracy trials against unions in the second half of the nineteenth century than before the decision in *Commonwealth v. Hunt*.[44] What eventually ended them, more than a change of attitude by government or business, was the reluctance of juries, more and more constituted by working people, to convict unions on conspiracy charges. *Commonwealth v. Hunt* was even more remarkable in the trek of labour history on this continent, since Judge Lemuel Shaw (in the Supreme Judicial Court of Massachusetts) found legal a strike by shoemakers called to force an employer to dismiss a scab. Canada again dragged behind the thinking of the times. It was 31 years after an American court dissolved the identity between conspiracy theory and unions before Canadian law did the same.

As late as 1872, striking newspaper printers at George Brown's Toronto *Globe* were prosecuted for criminal conspiracy "in restraint of trade".[45] In the same year, the printers' union in Stockholm signed without a strike its first contract with an organization of print-shop owners.[46]

When the criminal conspiracy tactic no longer worked, business and government looked for new methods of fighting unions. Measures to stop the growth of the Industrial Workers of the World, the "Wobblies", included such extreme attacks that a group of distinguished lawyers in the United States, including Felix Frankfurter, denounced the Attorney General, A. Mitchell Palmer. In a pamphlet published by the American Civil Liberties Union, the lawyers accused the Justice Department of committing "continual illegal acts" against the Wobblies. This was done, they said, "under the guise of a campaign for the suppression of radical activities".[47]

The I.W.W., the continent's first industrial union, had wide appeal among the unskilled working classes, especially immigrants. Congress amended the immigration laws to allow virtual on-the-spot deportation of suspected anarchists, a bill aimed solely at the I.W.W. The Postmaster-General banned I.W.W. literature from the mails. Federal Bureau of Investigation agents raided I.W.W. union offices and planted spies in I.W.W. locals. The press incited hysteria against the Wobblies, a role the media still act out for foes of organized labour.

A San Francisco newspaper headline in 1918 said: "Kaiser's Coin Pays for I.W.W. Sabotage." An Indianapolis newspaper headline the following year flared: "Bolsheviki and I.W.W.'s Planned U.S. Revolution." But "no case of an I.W.W. saboteur caught practising sabotage or convicted" is known.[48]

(The raids against the I.W.W., the mass arrests and incommunicado interrogation that characterized them, were carried out under the direction of the young head of the U.S. Justice Department's General Intelligence Division, J. Edgar Hoover.)

The spillover of anti-union hatred and I.W.W. paranoia across the border was to be expected. Though the I.W.W. claimed 10,000 members in Canada in 1911, it declined rapidly soon afterwards and was outlawed across the country in 1918.[49]

But conspiracy charges failed to crush the labour movement. Blatant denial of fundamental civil rights, such as the tactics used against the Wobblies, became unpalatable to the public. A new weapon was needed to bolster anti-union corporations and defend the practice of strikebreaking. "The technique should meet the requirements of speed, simplicity, and . . . above all, if employers were to resist organization of their firms it was mandatory to remove the labour dispute from the jurisdiction of a potentially sympathetic jury. All these requirements were met by the labour injunction".[50]

Though obviously damaging in its effect on union resistance to strikebreaking, the court injunction limiting or outlawing picketing outside a struck company was ubiquitous until quite recently. Only in this decade, really, have the courts begun hesitantly to curtail the service of issuing injunctions almost automatically at the request of an employer's legal counsel.

The use of an injunction to break legal strikes became a turbulent political issue in a confrontation between the labour movement and the Progressive-Conservative government of

Ontario in 1966. Late in 1965, the Textile Workers' Union of America struck Tilco Plastics Limited in Peterborough. Five days after the strike began, an injunction limiting pickets to eight was issued. It was defied, and Attorney-General Arthur Wishart intervened personally. His department, with motion pictures and still photographs, prepared a case against 28 unionists for contempt of court.

Ontario Supreme Court Chief Justice G. A. Gale found 26 guilty of defying a court order. He defended the use of injunctions, quoting the law, which allowed injunctions *ex parte*, literally on the complaint of one side, for up to four days if the courts are satisfied "a breach of the peace . . . injury . . . or damage to property has occurred or is likely to occur".[51]

Twenty-five unionists got jail sentences from Gale, from 15 days to two months. The opposition parties in the legislature and the official labour movement screamed. Lawyer Elmer Sopha, Liberal party member from Sudbury at the time, said the jailed unionists were "victims of an unjust law that no longer fits this enlightened age". Managements were "running to the court to get injunctions", Sopha said, and gained "a material advantage over the striker".[52]

Another Liberal, lawyer Leonard Braithwaite of Etobicoke, said the root of labour's conflict with the judicial system is that judges are isolated from workers. "Apart from the fact that judges are generally unlikely to be drawn from the ranks of labour's sympathizers," Braithwaite said, "they are often men whose social and economic education was completed 30 or 40 years ago—at a time when collective bargaining was much less understood than it is today."[53]

Although Mr. Justice Gale disputed "as vigorously as I can" the contention that courts hand injunctions to managements "as a matter of course", the Labour Department's own study of the weapon revealed that 222 *ex parte* injunctions were issued in the eight-year period of 1958 to 1966.[54]

Central to the injunction debate was the fairness of the *ex parte* process, which let management lawyers into court without the striking unionists even being aware of it (and lawyers did this in 178 injunctions). The courts could "make a determination of disputed questions of fact on hearsay evidence, which experience has taught is so often untrustworthy that it is inadmissible at a trial. . . ."[55] The judges typically relied solely on affidavits submitted by management without "any opportunity of observing the witness".[56]

Property rights were supreme. Arguments that peaceful

picketing is part of a basic civil liberty, that of free speech and assembly, were rejected. The pro-business bias of the courts was evident. Picketing to urge a boycott to support a strike in 1963 was banned by a judge who said the boycott would benefit only "a particular class", while the right of management to unrestricted trade "is a right far more fundamental and of far greater importance . . . and is for the benefit of the community at large".[57]

Another judge was even more extreme, saying "the common law right to peacefully communicate information by picketing with placards must stand some revision in our day and age. . . ." He observed further that if picketing interfered with moving goods from struck plants, it would constitute "a conspiracy and a nuisance. . . ."[58]

Until the labour movement packed picket lines and defied injunctions at Tilco Plastics and at the Oshawa *Times* strike in January and February, 1966, there was little public furore over *ex parte* injunctions. The government had ignored its own Select Committee on Labour Relations in the Legislature, a committee dominated by Conservatives, which recommended in 1958 that no *ex parte* injunctions be issued in labour disputes. It was not until 12 years later that at last the government amended the Judicature Act to ban *ex parte* injunctions except in defined emergencies.

Injunctions are still a feature of Canadian industrial relations, although the recent amendments to the Judicature Act tighten up considerably the conditions and procedures for management to get them. All a company still has to do is convince a judge that disorder is possible. Other facts are irrelevant. As Canadian professor Leo Johnson said in 1971, "The fact that the reason that violence occurs is that the owner is bringing in strike-breakers to take the workers' jobs, and that these scabs are assisted by the local police, has no bearing on the [judge's] decision."

The injunction debate was not Ontario's solely. In the period 1955 to 1965, British Columbia judges handed down more than 300 injunctions in labour-management disputes.[59] Some were ludicrous. One B.C. judge was so enthusiastic he outlawed congregations of three or more strikers within 600 feet of a plant entrance. His range also took in the headquarters of the striking union, legally preventing more than three members from occupying the building simultaneously.[60]

Far from being impressed by free-speech arguments from the unions, judges flouted the concept. One ordered in his injunction in 1962 that the pickets had to say to strikebreakers "they were at liberty to work without fear of reprisals or expulsion. . . ."[61] Another, two years later, compelled strikers to tell customers of the struck company that the union would allow their management "to deal with that customer without reprisal".[62] (But it doesn't appear that a Canadian judge has gone as far as one American court did several years ago, with an injunction ordering pickets not to speak at all.)

Friends of the unionists argued futilely against the injunction. "The law of injunctions was never intended to apply to labour disputes," said MP David Lewis, now federal leader of the New Democratic Party, in 1966. "It was intended to be applied only in civil matters involving property differences between citizens. . . . Let us change the law so that [the courts] will not be able to use an injunction order, in effect, to break strikes . . . to force people to work . . . to interfere with the bargaining process and the rights of Canadian workers."[63]

The provincial government held fast. Attorney-General Wishart was not impressed when opposition party members reminded him that most legislatures in the United States had prohibited the courts from issuing injunctions in labour disputes decades earlier. When MPP James Renwick of the New Democratic Party debated the government in 1969, he said Wishart "gets terribly upset because he haled the people in Peterborough into the court to cover up the fact that he had not effectively dealt with the Oshawa *Times* strike". Wishart interjected, "I just want to make it clear I was never upset".[64]

The controversial Royal Commission Inquiry into Labour Disputes headed by Justice Ivan C. Rand also recommended in 1968 that *ex parte* injunctions be outlawed. The Rand Report dispelled one prevalent myth about violence on the picket line. In a 10-year period of strikes and lockouts reviewed by Rand, employers reported actual damage or injuries in just 12.2 per cent of the disputes. Yet the police were summoned in 42 per cent of the strikes.[65] It could be asked why the police were summoned so routinely, if not to intimidate the strikers.

Rand's researchers found that of 407 strikes and lockouts where information could be obtained, strikebreakers had been used in almost 30 per cent. In no surprising conclusion, they found that smaller employers use strikebreakers more often and more successfully than large companies. Three-quarters of such instances involved operations of fewer than 75 empoyees.[66]

Rand also discounted the myth of union power. Employers shut their operations completely in just a little over half the strikes and lockouts. What Rand called "a mere" 7.8 per cent of nearly 800 companies involved in strikes achieved full operation with strikebreakers.[67] Rand calculated that "possibly . . . where strikers number over 75 it is impractical to try to replace such a number with outside replacements",[68] although in more than 30 other broken strikes greater numbers of strikebreakers were successfully and in management's view "practically" recruited.

If 75 empoyees is an average number of unionists who lost their jobs to strikebreakers in each broken strike between 1958 and 1967, it can be estimated that more than 4,500 workers who wanted a union were denied one. A survey of affiliates conducted by the Ontario Federation of Labour in early 1972 showed that at least 50 strikes have been broken with strikebreakers since 1965. Even if only 50 employees on the average were involved in each strike, then 2,500 workers in Ontario have had their bargaining rights stolen by strikebreakers in the past seven years.[69]

Leniency by the courts and restraint by government in their traditional aggressive enforcement of injunctions against unions has eased only in the past year or two. It was almost extraordinary when a judge refused an injunction in 1971 against Toronto longshoremen who were supporting a boycott called by the International Brotherhood of Teamsters.

A trucking company called Truk-King Limited was using temporary labour to drive cartage off the Toronto harbour docks. Since the drivers were contract labour, not employees, the company could not legally be organized by the Teamsters. The trucking concern was linked in business with a private stevedoring and warehousing business on the harbour. The harbour contact tipped off trucking company officials on incoming cargo. Using below-union-wage labour, the company began undercutting the unionized cartage firms on the docks. To combat the boycott, the company asked for an injunction against the longshoremen, who were refusing to load Truk-King trailers. The company asserted it was suffering irreparable harm and that the boycott was a conspiracy to interfere with the company's right to conduct its business.

Justice Patrick Galligan of the Ontario Supreme Court refused, contending Truk-King "has deliberately so organized its affairs that it must have foreseen that the inevitable result would be . . . a labour dispute in an important public enterprise. . . . To extricate itself from the present difficulties it is argued that the plaintiff may have to take steps which may result in its becoming unionized. If this should happen, far from saying it is irreparable harm, I am not satisfied that it is even harm."

What marked Galligan's departure from the entire thrust of labour relations in the courts until that time was his decision: "I am not prepared to say in this day and age that in all cases an agreement by union members to generally further legitimate trade union goals is a conspiracy that founds a right to damages, even though the effect of such an agreement may be to affect the business interests of a third party."

If at last the doors to "justice" that have been used to close out unions for so long are being shut on managements, there still exists the right of management to repel any infringement on its prerogatives by using professional strikebreakers.

Strikeguards, industrial spies and professional strikebreaking agencies operate without hindrance in Ontario and other parts of Canada. Only in Canada.

Notes

1. *Violations of Free Speech and Rights of Labor*, Report of the U.S. Senate Committee on Education and Labor (La Follette committee), Report No. 6, 1939.
2. An economist with the National Labor Relations Board estimated that the incomes of the top three detective agencies conducting strikebreaking work and anti-union espionage in the 1930's amounted to $60 million a year. They employed 135,000 industrial spies. Cited in "Industrial Strikebreaking—The Byrnes Act," *University of Chicago Law Review*, 1937, p. 658.
3. Alaska, Arkansas, California, Colorado, Connecticut, Delaware, Hawaii, Idaho, Indiana, Iowa, Kansas, Kentucky, Louisiana, Maine, Maryland, Massachusetts, Michigan, Minnesota, Mississippi, Missouri, Montana, Nebraska, New Hampshire, New Jersey, New York, North Dakota, Ohio, Oklahoma, Oregon, Pennsylvania, Rhode Island, South Carolina, South Dakota, Tennessee, Texas, Utah, Washington, West Virginia, Wisconsin, Wyoming. Cities can pass their own labour-standards laws in the United States. Separate municipal ordinances outlawing professional strikebreaking cover 44.8 million persons, according to 1970 census figures. State anti-strikebreaking legislation covers one-quarter of the country's population, 54,349,000.
4. Wolff, Leon, "Battle at Homestead," *American Heritage*, April, 1965, pp. 64-79.
5. Levinson, Edward, "Strikebreaking Incorporated," *Harper's Monthly Magazine*, 1935, p. 720.
6. *Ibid.*, p. 724.
7. Jamieson, Stuart, *Times of Trouble: Labour Unrest In Canada, 1900-1967*, Queen's Printer, Ottawa, 1971, p. 8.

8. Jamieson, *op. cit.*, p. 101.
9. Cited in Jamieson, *op. cit.*, p. 123.
10. *Information,* publication of the United Steelworkers of America, May 1968, p. 6.
11. *Ibid.,* p. 27.
12. *Ibid.,* p. 23.
13. *Ibid.,* p. 22.
14. *Legislature of Ontario Debates,* *(Hansard),* February 15, 1963, p. 782.
15. Taylor, Benjamin J., and Witney, Fred, *Labour Relations Law,* Prentice-Hall, Inc., Englewood Cliffs, N. J., 1971, p. 118.
16. La Follette, *Report on Industrial Espionage,* Report No. 46, Part 3, 75th Congress, p. 22.
17. "Congress Assails Industrial Thuggery," *University of Pennsylvania Law Review,* February, 1937, p. 407.
18. McDiarmid, Garnet, and Pratt, David, *Teaching Prejudice,* Ontario Institute for Studies in Education, 1971, p. 99.
19. *Ibid.,* p. 97.
20. Although Canada's labour laws are tougher on unions than American labour legislation, the Canadian public believes they aren't tough enough. And public opinion is hardening, according to the Canadian Institute of Public Opinion (The Gallup Poll of Canada). In 1966, a national survey concluded that 33 per cent of the public believe laws regarding unions are not strict enough. Four years later the percentage favouring tougher laws rose to 50 per cent. Asking which is the "biggest threat" to the country, big business or big labour, the pollsters found (in 1969) 34 per cent of all Canadians believe it's labour, 23 per cent government and only 18 per cent business. In the United States, by comparison, 46 per cent of the population believe big business is the greatest threat. Whether this is the result of a generally more favourable climate for union activity created by the government is open to speculation. In Canada, 66 per cent said in 1961 they approve "in general" of labour unions. In 1970 the number giving approval declined to 54.

    There is evidence of a lack of knowledge about unions, perhaps to be credited to the mass media, which whip up anti-union feeling but provide little factual information about how unions operate. A study prepared for the Federal Task Force on Labour Relations reveals that when Gallup interviewers asked the names of unions "you had in mind," 20 per cent of the critics couldn't name one. Sixteen per cent "damned 'all them' unions."
21. *Hansard,* May 27, 1969, p. 4925.
22. Jamieson, *op. cit.,* p. 347.
23. Bernstein, Irving, "State Public Utility Laws and Mediation," *Labour Law Journal,* August, 1956, p. 500.
24. Bok, Derek C., and Dunlop, John T., *Labour and the American Community,* Simon & Shuster, 1970, (cited in *Panel,* publication of the University of San Francisco Labour-Management School, January-February, 1970, Vol. 20, No. 3.)
25. *Ibid.*
26. *Ibid.*
27. "Strikes and Lockouts in Canada and other Countries," *Labour Gazette,* Canada Department of Labour, Vol. 31, 1931, p. 138.
28. Jamieson, *op. cit.,* p. 25.

29. Cited in Jamieson, *op. cit.*, pp. 52-53.
30. Schuster, E. J. E., *Industrial Conflict and Its Institutionalization: A Comparative Analysis, of Sweden, Canada, and the United States,* Ph.d. thesis, 1970, University of Oregon, p. 338.
31. Schuster, *op. cit.*, pp. 312-318.
32. *Ibid.*, p. 173.
33. *Ibid.*, p. 248.
34. Samuelson, Kurt, "The Ironminers' Walkout—Signal of Change?" *Viewpoint,* Jan. 28, 1970, p. 1.
35. Jamieson, *op. cit.*, p. 56.
36. *Fortune,* January, 1935, p. 59.
37. *The University of Chicago Law Review, op cit.,* p. 659.
38. *University of Pennsylvania Law Review, op. cit.,* p. 409.
39. In the strike against Texpack Limited in Brantford, Ontario, in 1971, policemen for a day refused to supply protection to buses of strikebreakers, an episode that stands alone in labour history in Ontario and probably in all the rest of the country.
40. Jamieson, *op. cit.*, p. 58.
41. Cited in Jamieson, *op. cit.*, p. 69.
42. *Ibid.*, p. 76.
43. Taylor and Witney, *op. cit.*, p. 21.
44. *Ibid.*, p. 22.
45. Montague, J. T., et al., "The Growth of Labour Organizations in Canada, 1900-1950: The Rise of Trade Unions to Their Present Strength and Influence," *Labour Gazette,* Vol. 15, No. 9, September, 1950, pp. 1398-1390.
46. Schuster, *op. cit.*, p. 250.
47. Frankfurter, Felix, et al., *"To the American People—Report on the Illegal Practices of the United States Department of Justice,* New York, A.C.L.U., 1920.
48. Dowell, Eldrige, R., *A History of Criminal Syndicalism Legislation in the United States,* De Capo, 1969, p. 36.
49. Schuster, *op. cit.*, p. 185.
50. Taylor and Witney, *op. cit.*, p. 23.
51. Carrothers, A. W. R., and Palmer, E. E., *Report of a Study on the Labour Injunction in Ontario,* Ontario Department of Labour, October, 1966, p. 333.
52. *Ibid.*, p. 335.
53. *Ibid.*, pp. 346-347.
54. *Ibid.*, p. 87.
55. *Ibid.*, p. 25.
56. *Ibid.*
57. *Ibid.*, p. 27.
58. *Ibid.*, pp. 45-46.
59. *Ibid.*, p. 349.
60. Cutler, Philip, *Labour Relations and Court Review: A Study in the Supervision and Control of Administrative Tribunals,* Tundra Books, 1968, Montreal, 1968, (not paginated).
61. Carrothers and Palmer, *op. cit.*, p. 98.
62. *Ibid.*
63. *The Globe and Mail,* June 23, 1966.
64. *Hansard,* June 2, 1969, p. 5161.
65. *Report of the Royal Commission Inquiry into Labour Disputes,* Queen's Printer, Toronto, August, 1968, p. 181.

21

66. *Ibid.*, p. 178.
67. *Ibid.*, p. 172.
68. *Ibid.*, p. 178.
69. The survey was supplemented by research from federal Labour Department statistics. Nearly 200 replies to the O.F.L. questionnaire were received. Until 1968 the Labour Department recorded all strikes, but since then has only kept statistics on disputes involving 100 employees or more. This statistical difference means the employers most likely to break unions will not appear in the records of the Labour Department.

2

The Rise of
Richard Grange

Commercialized strike services tend to produce violence and disorder. Such violence comes partly as a result of the natural hostility of workingmen against the use of industrial mercenaries, but is more directly attributable to the activities of professional strike followers and the employers who use them.

Report of the U.S. Senate Committee on Education and Labour, 1939.

Richard Grange didn't ask for the publicity he got unexpectedly in 1971, when the leader of the New Democratic Party read one of Grange's sales letters to the Legislature of Ontario. Not that Grange dislikes the notoriety his career has given him. He is perhaps the only strikebreaker in Canada with his own public-relations man. Pearl Bergoff, the flamboyant American scab lord, also had a PR man, who had once been secretary to New York City's police commissioner.[1] Grange's publicist is James Tannian, former director of public relations for the Ontario Workmen's Compensation Board, where he reportedly was well paid for a young man (he is in his 30s), at more than $22,000 a year. Tannian left the board and in 1972 was with Public & Industrial Relations Limited (P.I.R.) in Toronto. International Nickel Company of Canada Limited and the Toronto Construction Association, the contractors' lobby, are other P.I.R. clients.

Grange's sales letter was startling. He openly boasted that 40 companies had used the "services" of his Canadian Driver Pool Limited and that "with our aid, these companies broke the strikes. . . ."

The claim of having broken so many strikes was, like much of the contents of the three-page letter, untrue.

Untrue was the claim that "through research and experimentation" Canadian Driver Pool had learned "many different methods of bringing about a fair settlement". Untrue was the claim that Driver Pool had "a separate security division". Untrue was the assertion that "these men have been trained especially for this type of work". Untrue was the statement that Driver Pool had Doberman pinschers "which are trained for crowd control and plant security". (It was true there were Dobermans, but none was trained, only housebroken.)

Untrue, too, was the impression left by the abstract royal-blue-and-white letterhead that there was a real company called Canadian Driver Pool Limited. At the time the first batch of letters went out in mid-1970, former employees say, no such company existed—except in the mind of Richard Grange.

The letter said "our company was formed two years ago due to circumstances which necessitated the formation of an organized Company, which could offer specialized services to a strike-bound Company". In fact, two years before Grange had only a cartage company, Cart-Rite Cartage Limited.

He did not bother incorporating and registering the company and name Driver Pool until September, 1970—two years after he was claiming C.D.P. went into business.

The dogs turned into more of an embarrassment than an effective tool against the unions. One former strikebreaker employed by Grange recalls taking Grange's Doberman Troll on strike work one night, and the dog wouldn't let him back into his car. Grange loved the dogs, though. Former employees swear he slept with a dog and would leave the engine of his car running on cold nights to keep the animals warm while they guarded Grange's clients. He also took them to parties. The dogs probably terrified more Driver Pool employees than strikers. Grange let them roam freely around the warehouses where his cartage business and C.D.P. operated. "If you made a wrong move," says a former Grange employee, "you got a dog around your neck."

Starting with the first batch of letters to company presidents, Grange built up his strikebreaking business, a racket he got into almost by accident.

In 1970 Toronto milk-truck drivers went on strike. An official of Durham Transport Limited, which regularly hauled milk from suppliers to major dairies, called on Grange for extra trucks and drivers. Grange supplied them. Although Grange now takes credit for breaking the strike by members of the International Brotherhood of Teamsters, in truth his role was minor. The Teamsters got practically the settlement they wanted.²

The five trucks Grange supplied for Dominion Dairies Limited and other struck dairies were from the small local cartage business that Grange and former friends had set up a year earlier, called Cart-Rite Cartage Limited. Grange's relationship with Durham Transport was helpful in other ways. Former drivers say a man at Durham had a contact in the provincial Transport Department and could tip them off to which weight scales were open on provincial highways. Overloaded trucks can be ordered off the roads. Trucks driven for Grange could be sneaked to alternative routes to avoid detection.

It is typical of Grange to be eclectic in his business. He grabs what he can—drivers, ideas, names—from clients and associates. A manual for employers that is used by Canadian Driver Pool is based in large part on a guidebook for supervisors prepared by Irwin Toy Limited in Toronto, which broke a lengthy strike that started in 1971—without Driver Pool's help. Even the name for Cart-Rite Cartage, recalls a former partner, occurred to Grange while he was watching the television show "Bonanza". The heros are the Cartwright family.

Canadian Driver Pool, the name and the idea, were borrowed from competitors. Grange also took their men.

A company Grange worked alongside to break an independent union of drivers at W. J. Mowat Cartage Company in Toronto in 1970 was Extra Driver Services. Extra Driver used to exist as just a number and name in the telephone book. Correspondence went to a post office box. Today the strikebreaking racket is more extroverted, thanks in part to Grange. Extra Driver now lists an address. The owner of Extra Driver is Lorne E. Taylor of Brampton, Ontario, who also is president of Dufferin Car & Truck Rentals Limited. Both companies are run from 131 Cartwright Avenue in Toronto.

Leonard Yates, a partner in Grange's Intercontinental Container Leasing Limited, was a supervisor at Transport International Pool, a trucking company that won't refuse strike business. T.I.P. used to rent truck trailers to Cart-Rite.

Grange decided to set up his own "separate security division" after working strikes with Anning Investigations Limited (since taken over by the American security giant, Wackenhut Corporation).

Driver Pool itself was set up to circumvent the Public Commercial Vehicles Act. Inter-city trucking licenses are hard to get. The provincial Transport Department controls trucking in Ontario. Without pull, it's tough to get a cartage license in the already overcrowded and fiercely competitive business.

Without pull, people can still go into the cartage business as Grange did, setting up one company to lease drivers and another to rent trucks. Driver Pool was incorporated August 11, 1970, and Intercontinental Container Leasing Limited on September 3 of the same year.

Grange sold his business aggressively. It wasn't too hard. Down the street from Cart-Rite's office at 278 Bridgeland in Downsview in northern Metropolitan Toronto was Horn's Provisioners Limited. Horn's rents freezers to the public, then keeps the appliances stocked with foods. One of Grange's oldest contracts is delivering for Horn's. He walked in and got the business.

He also got a partner, Horn's president, James A. P. Patry. Patry built a reputation in the food industry by taking over a small company going nowhere, Twentieth Century Foods, amalgamating his operations and making a lot of money. He entertains Grange on the Patry yacht. A former strikebreaker recalls that Grange told him Patry is "a guy who can help us a lot". Grange made Patry a vice-president of Driver Pool. A former Driver Pool trooper describes Patry as "a real wheeler-dealer".

Friends helped out, too. They referred business to Grange. But mostly he sold himself.

"Rick's a fantastic salesman," says an ex-strikebreaker who set up Cart-Rite. "He's just got it. He's a fantastic salesman. He's very presentable. People like him automatically."

There is a lot to like. Tall, slim, not a trace of beard, bespectacled, Grange could pass for a stockbroker or a college student. He dresses well, but not flamboyantly, in high-fashion clothes. He impressed Sayvette's and got their cartage business. He impressed Canadian General Electric, and got theirs. He impressed Fry-Cadbury, the baking corporation, and got their business. He hauled for Clairtone Sound Corporation. Jim Patry of Horn's branched out and bought a franchise for an automatic liquor dispenser called Bar-Boy. Grange's men installed them in swank restaurants and motels.

Grange's reputation was spreading. He was dealing with some of the biggest companies in the country. His trucks were running cargo out and strikebreakers in for corporations in the petroleum industry (Veedol Oil), electrical products (Trane Company of Canada and Pioneer Electric), modular construction (Pre-Con Murray, part of the big St. Mary's

Cement conglomerate), chemicals (Union Carbide), automotive products (Chrysler Airtemp), computers (Honeywell Controls), construction (National Sewer Pipe and Canadian Phoenix Steel & Pipe) and precious metals (Johnson, Matthey & Mallory).

Specializing in strike work had an unlimited future. "He was starting to see how lucrative the strikebreaking thing was," says a one-time associate who used to do Grange's books.

As he got bigger, he got bolder. He would ask for $10,000 retainers from a company before going into a strike. Some say he got it, some deny it.

As he got bigger, he also got more aloof from his men. They were well paid but worked tortuous hours. Some grossed $400 a week. But they drove up to 80 hours a week and longer and risked the picket-line confrontations that Driver Pool had provoked.

A partner in Cart-Rite says Grange is admired, thanked and disliked all at once by his gang. They know, he says, that "Rick doesn't give a damn—he doesn't drive through the picket lines."

He paid himself up to $250 a week with the company's money from Driver Pool and bought himself a grey Corvette. (Originally Grange was treasurer of Driver Pool and he called his wife, Marilyn, the president. Now he calls himself president.)

He continued to frequent Granny's, long his favourite hangout. He would spend fabulous amounts of money at this downtown "swingles" bar. Friends remember tabs worth hundreds of dollars in a single night. He bought drinks for the band, for strangers, for everyone. He was such a good customer at Granny's that the *maitre d'* held Grange's favourite table for him. He met young stockbrokers there and played the market. He got introduced to the owner, J. Douglas Crashley. Crashley was the kind of prominent acquaintance Grange liked and courted. Crashley's connections include Elgin Motors (president), the Walker House and Ascot Hotels (owner), Toronto Citizens Redevelopment Advisory Board (chairman), Toronto Planning Board (past chairman), and Central Precision Limited (president), a company that repairs car engines. This prominent civic leader became a customer of Driver Pool's services in 1972. Crashley's Central Precision, in the northwestern Rexdale section of Metropolitan Toronto, was the scene of perhaps Grange's most violent strike work.

By the middle of 1971, Grange's operations were generating

an $8,000 weekly payroll. Cheques for $4,000, $5,000 and $6,000 were coming in from his clients.

Not only was the take high, so was the overhead. Grange bought four trailers at $7,000 apiece and ordered new tractors to pull them at $22,000 a cab.

His network expanded. He moved the operation to a new warehouse at 35 Oak Street in Weston in the northwest quadrant of Metro Toronto. He signed a two-year lease from the United Dairy and Poultry Co-operative Limited, which sells Gay-Lea products.

Grange declared he had a new company, Pro-Con Consolidated Warehousing, with himself as president, and he had his other companies pay rent to it. He called Pro-Con a limited company and got his friends to invest in it. Later Grange declared it to be a subsidiary of Cart-Rite Cartage. Until April, 1972, there was no record of Pro-Con Consolidated Warehousing in the Companies Branch of the Ontario Department of Financial and Commercial Affairs, and two of the original directors of Cart-Rite deny Pro-Con ever had legal ties with Cart-Rite. Cars were registered to Pro-Con Consolidated Warehousing "Limited". Other business, like insurance, was paid under the same phoney name, despite the existence of corporation law to prevent unauthorized use of the term "limited".

Grange used his father-in-law, H. Robert Bertram, to get his first major strike work, with Honeywell Controls. The Scarborough, Ontario plant claimed it reached 80 per cent of normal production while Grange's trucks and drivers shipped the goods made by strikebreakers. Metro Toronto policemen, some on horseback, kept the picket lines orderly.

His father, Alfred E. Grange, until recently a high official at the Toronto headquarters of the Canadian Imperial Bank of Commerce, was used as the operation's first auditor. Cart-Rite had started, in fact, with just a telephone in the basement of the elder Grange's house in a wealthy neighbourhood of Don Mills in suburban Metro.

Grange's business sprouted so quickly that his clients' demands outdistanced his supply of equipment. Handling sometimes four strikes at once, he needed to rent trucks and trailers from other sources. He turned to Avis, Auto-hire (a subsidiary of the big Maislin Transport operation), Rent-way, Dufferin Truck Rental, Triad Trucklease and Transport International Pool. Some were overjoyed at their new business. Some lost their infatuation, like Avis, which reportedly refused to rent

Grange any more equipment when the agency learned their trucks were being used for strikebreaking.

Former employees say Grange took advantage of the captive clients who hired him to do their strikebreaking. Sometimes the rent-a-truck firms jacked up their normal prices as much as 10 per cent and paid Grange an equal kick-back. The struck companies paid the leasing bill, because Grange told them to. He pocketed the bonuses. The whole rake-off was legal. Perhaps, one ex-partner acknowledges, it is "unethical".

His letters to company presidents, his personal calls at their offices (often unannounced) seem farcical to his own friends who helped him. "It was strictly bullshit," says one. "He talked about professional truck drivers, professional dog handlers, professional cameramen. Everything was 'professional.' He even told them he had infra-red cameras for night photography."

Photography has a special meaning for Grange's gang. His promotional letters say the "security team" will "record any acts which could be detrimental in any way to your company".

For executives who don't get the point, he thoughtfully elaborates that "this information is useful in presenting a case with regard to an injunction against the union".

Some strikers have started "photographing back" at Driver Pool strikeguards. Generally Grange's mercenaries don't like it.

Strikers think the photography is just harassment. Terry Ribeca, president of the United Steelworkers local at Kenroc Tools Limited in Toronto, says strikers know the camera can lie. He and 80 others strikers at Kenroc faced Grange cameras, trucks and scab herders for several weeks in 1971. "For example, say if I punched somebody on the face," says Ribeca, "they would have a picture of me punching someone on the face. But they wouldn't have the other scene. Maybe he punched me first. What they actually get is a one-sided thing."

If a man with a camera followed any other citizen, the unflattered subject might have grounds for a charge of mischief against the nuisance. The public, however, has been trained to accept curbs on the freedom of unions and their members that would not be tolerated on the street if there were no picket line present. "There is no need to photograph peaceful picketing," says American management consultant LeRoy Marseau in his book, *Dealing with a Union*. Taking pictures of strikers the way Driver Pool lensmen do, for lack of anything better to do, might be considered by the U.S. National Labour Relations Board, "to be evidence of improper employer motives" says Marceau.

Policemen at Gidon Industries Limited, a muffler manufacturer in Toronto that employed Grange in 1972, told strikers, "There's nothing illegal about taking pictures." There is, apparently, in flashing hand-held mirrors to reflect sunlight into the eyes of Grange's cameramen. Members of the United Steelworkers of America at Gidon were threatened with arrest if they did not desist from doing this in self-defence. At Union Carbide Canada Limited, another Grange client, pickets of the Oil, Chemical and Atomic Workers' International Union were told the same by Oakville, Ontario, policemen. At Gidon the strikeguard-photographers sat in Grange's station wagons or patrolled company property. At Union Carbide, the company generously gave the cameraman an inside perch behind a window.

A writer in 1934 in an American magazine remarked, "It is always a source of wonder that impoverished manufacturers, insisting that they cannot possibly afford to raise wages, can nevertheless see their way clear to spending exorbitant sums on strikebreakers."[3]

It should not be astounding that big and respected companies would engage private armies in the second half of the twentieth century for the dirty business of strikebreaking. The La Follette committee that probed strikebreaking in the United States in the late 1930's found the same thing. Many blue-chip corporations of the day used strikebreakers (as some do today). Pinkerton's biggest client was General Motors, which paid out $839,764 for spies and strikebreakers between 1934 and 1936, most of it to the Pinkerton agency.[4] Standard Oil Company paid Pearl Bergoff $175,000 for two weeks' work in 1929.[5] Other customers of the strikebreaking rackets included International Harvester, Goodyear Tire and Rubber, Westinghouse, Du Pont, U.S. Rubber (Uniroyal), American Telephone and Telegraph, Continental Can, U.S. Steel (successor to Carnegie's Homestead, Pennsylvania, operations), Chrysler, Firestone Tire and Rubber, Kraft, Kelvinator, the Borden Milk Co., R.C.A., William Wrigley, Quaker Oats, American Can, Libby-Owens Glass, Curtis Publishing and Campbell Soup.

In similar fashion, Grange has all sizes of companies, from multi-national corporations and domestic corporate mesomorphs down to small manufacturers, eating up his stories and praising his services.

What they get is sometimes not what they pay for. Professional strikebreaking expenses are tax-deductible, however. Grange's sales pitch stresses protection. He will also oblige by comforting executives with peace of mind. Some standard advice is to let Grange's men check office telephone lines and the homes of key company personnel for wiretaps. This was part of the service Redpath Sugars Limited was given for the $75,000 the company paid Grange in 1971 during a strike by the International Chemical Workers' Union. Kimberly-Clark of Canada also had the homes and offices of chief executives "debugged" during a strike by the International Brotherhood of Pulp, Sulphite and Paper Mill Workers in 1971 at its St. Catharines, Ontario, plant.

Grange sends in a man with a device called an R.F. Detector (for radio frequency). The apparatus picks up FM radio signals, the type emitted from concealed, wireless microphones. Pioneer Electric also had its offices checked for bugs by Driver Pool during a strike by the United Electrical, Radio and Machine Workers of America at Toronto in 1971. The same year so did Kenroc Tools in Toronto during a United Steelworkers of America strike.

No "bugs" were found. One Driver Pool operator of the R.F. admits he didn't know how the detector worked and wouldn't know what to do if the mechanism ever found an electronic eavesdropper. Kimberly-Clark paid Grange nearly $4,400 for that advice and some additional consultation on security. He invoiced the company for "trucking services". There were no trucking services.

Ripping off the client is an old practice in the profession of strikebreaking. Agents recruited to break transit strikes by American scab king Pearl Bergoff routinely pocketed the fares when they drove streetcars and trolley buses.[6] The scab motormen drove the routes *they* wanted—not the scheduled ones—to guarantee the most profitable runs.

The hysteria evoked in boardrooms by professional strikebreaking agencies, said the La Follette committee, permits "a maximum of fraud and deception". The U.S. senators observed, "In time of strike even large and carefully run corporations seem to experience a collapse of proper accounting procedure, and vast sums are turned over to the leaders of the strikebreaking class without question or investigation."[7]

To promote their own business, strikebreaking agencies exposed by the committee had doctored the reports of industrial spies.[8] "The reports are usually 'edited' and sometimes 'built up' in the agency office before being passed on to the client," according to a journalist who covered the La Follette hearings.[9]

Multi-national corporations in Canada who employ Grange

and his competitors in the strikebreaking profession may only be importing the strategies of their American heritage. What motivates them to strikebreak is probably a feeling that the company's dignity is jeopardized if a corporate oligarch is rendered immobile in any of its various limbs by its own employees. What drives the small manufacturer to all-out attempts to smash unions is easier to see.

In many ways, the mastodon corporations are his enemy, too. But this does not make him a buddy to his employees, especially if they want to form a union. The small entrepreneur has devoured the myths a corporate-run world has told him about the wickedness of "big labour" and the threat of "big government". He feels suspicious, insecure, frustrated by much of the world around him. His own company may be the captive supplier of a giant corporation, which could take its business elsewhere and literally close him down.

In terms of basic business knowledge, he may not be astute. His own concern could be infested with inefficiency, waste and out-moded practices. The presence of a union attacks more of his prerogatives, crimps his freedom in his eyes and intensifies his alienation. Two political scientists, one from a Canadian university, one from an American school, believe "it is not surprising" that the small businessman's life "breeds a psychological environment conducive to manifestations of political extremism".[10] They confirmed their hypothesis in a survey of 121 small businessmen and 31 branch-plant managers in a western Canadian city.

Canadian branch-plant managers and other small businessmen have a natural affinity for the professional strikebreaker, who appears as a powerful saviour, who becomes a Robin Hood to the branch-plant managerial class.

Voting-pattern analysis in France confirms that small business gave support to the right-wing Poujadism movement that thrived in the 1950's.[11] And right-wing movements from the followers of Joseph McCarthy to the John Birch Society in the United States "have been heavily supported by small businessmen".[12]

Engaging a professional strikebreaker may be a way for the anguished businessman to "get off", as it were. Defying the picketing crowds outside his windows, the suffering little captain of industry hangs up the phone on the union negotiating committee and thinks, "You'll never get me alive."

One reason for the alienation of a branch-plant businessman could be that he listens to his own leaders. They have told him (and the public, through an eagerly servile mass media) that "big labour" is a menace not only to them and their profits but to the entire country.

There is a myth that businessmen talk themselves into believing that profits are secondary; fun is their real goal.

"Never before have I heard so many businessmen saying there is no fun in their jobs anymore," a vice-president of the Canadian Manufacturers' Association told a businessmen's luncheon in Galt, Ontario, in 1971.[13]

The president of Wiener Electric Limited, Daniel Wiener, who broke a Steelworkers' strike in 1969, said at the time, "Seventy per cent of manufacturers in Toronto are not in business for the money. They're working for pleasure and to keep people busy." He smashed the union rather than bargain with it and said he would close his plant and "live off my investments" before signing a contract.[14] (Wiener was convicted of unfair labour practices in violation of the Ontario Labour Relations Act and fined $200 for his corporate behaviour before the strike. A woman employee who tangled with a policeman as he was clearing a path for strikebreakers was also fined $200.)

The reaction of the small-business class to social benefits that a great number of Canadians take for granted is typified by the negotiator for Bach-Simpson Limited, which broke a strike by 90 employees that started in 1970. The plant manager, John Hinds, rejected the union committee's request for time off for an employee to attend the funeral of a close relative. According to University of Western Ontario sociologist James W. Rinehart, who studied the strike, Hinds said if the employees "really loved their relatives that much they would be living with them instead of working for Bach-Simpson".

Management leaders in Canada, in contrast to business leaders in the United States and elsewhere, campaign militantly against the labour movement. They have contributed to a hostile climate for collective bargaining and a fertile one for professional strikebreaking. Much of what they are saying is specious.

The conspiratorial way in which Canadian management lobbyists have gone about their anti-labour campaign clearly indicates their motives. The chief negotiators for Kimberly-Clark, Du Pont of Canada, the Steel Company of Canada, Noranda Mines and Algoma Steel pounded at unions with identical themes through 1970 and 1971. "These men, in their professional contacts, reached an informal meeting of minds . . . ," says *Financial Post* labour specialist Jack Schreiner.[15]

Others who joined the get-labour clique, according to Schreiner, were Noranda president Alfred Powis and Gulf Oil Canada Limited board chairman C. D. Shepard

Noranda negotiator R. Peter Riggin, an influential labour policy maker of the Canadian Chamber of Commerce, declared that 15 per cent of negotiated settlements at the bargaining table were being rejected by the rank and file. Asked for his source, he admitted he had read the figure in an American business magazine and assumed it applied equally to Canada.

Stelco's Harold Clawson gave the amazing opinion that "the balance of power of collective bargaining is now heavily on the side of unions". Ignoring the lengthy list of broken strikes in Ontario—almost all in plants of 100 employees or less—Clawson said the alleged imbalance favouring unions "is particularly so in the case of the small employer".

(Labour critic Ed Finn commented on the co-ordinated anti-labour mission's lament that governments favour unions, not companies, in current labour law: ". . . If they favour unions over employers, they have a strange way of showing it. The whole spectrum of recent government policy on labour relations, from Ottawa's wage guidelines to the jailing of labour leaders in Nova Scotia and British Columbia, has a decidedly anti-labour tinge."[16])

For whatever reason, the Canadian management class is not prepared to treat labour relations as honestly as businessmen in other industrialized countries. The American Management Association gives this advice to companies facing an organizing drive or a strike:

> Without taking up the cudgels either for or against continued operation, it can be said, however, that purely from the negotiating angle, and in particular from the standpoint of placing management in the most advantageous position at the bargaining table, the less strife and bitterness at the picket line the better.[17]

Riggin, in a speech at Chatham, Ontario, to a Rotary Club meeting, attacked the array of amendments to the Labour Relations Act introduced by the Ontario Tory government in 1970. For special mention he singled out a new feature in the law that raised the number of membership cards needed by union organizers to gain bargaining rights automatically—without a vote—from the Labour Relations Board, which sets the ground rules for collective bargaining in the province.

To try to deflate union resistance to the tougher certification procedures (up from 55 per cent membership in a bargaining unit to 65 per cent), the Tories dropped the percentage required to hold an election by the labour board.

Riggin called the new rules "a goodie for the unions. . . ."[18] In fact it was subtle union-busting because unions lose votes.

Between 1958 and 1965 unions gained certification automatically (when only 55 per cent of the plant or office had to be signed) in 70 per cent of the applications for bargaining rights before the labour board.[19] Between the beginning of 1964 and the end of 1969 unions were certified in nearly 83 per cent of the applications that followed surreptitious organizing drives.[20]

But unions won just 38 per cent of the votes held under the board's auspices in the first eight-year period.[21] They won barely 36 per cent in the years 1964-1969.[22]

Hardly a "goodie", the new rule meant managements could exert pressure where it counted, in the voting situations, and defeat union organizing drives in plant after plant.

Statistics gathered from the Ontario Labour Relations Board records indicate the tougher organizing ground rules are having a definite impact on the unions. Organizing has dropped to its lowest level in six years. In the first 12 months of organizing under the tougher procedures, 16,433 employees were successfully organized in unions certified by the Labour Board, compared to nearly 22,000 in the previous year and almost exactly the same number in the year before that—a decline of more than 25 per cent.

A favourite theme of the anti-union vagabonds is that time lost to strikes is intolerably high and damaging to the economy. The real costs, says economist Alan S. Carmel, in fact are "quite small". Most production, Carmel points out, is hardly "lost" at all. It is usually rescheduled after a strike has ended.

Unemployment at its 1971 rate of seven per cent, says Carmel, means the potential work lost is 14 times the amount lost by strikes. "Indeed," he concludes, "the time used for one lunch-time martini is at least as long as the time lost per week per worker due to strikes."[23]

The management crusaders had a juicy bit of anti-labour propaganda in 1970, after the previous year's figure for lost time caused by strikes showed a record number of man-days, 7.3 million. The figure led Algoma Steel's Donald A. Machum, the company's chief negotiator, to declare, "Collective bargaining in Canada today is a very sick institution."[24]

But the time lost in 1969 to industrial accidents in just one province—Ontario—was half the lost time caused by strikes in the entire country. According to the Ontario Workmen's Compensation Board, disabling injuries cost industry and employees 3,485,669 man-days of work in 1969.

What Machum and his friends failed consistently to point out was that most of the time off caused by strikes occurred in three major walkouts: International Nickel Company of Canada, Machum's Algoma Steel and Harold Clawson's Stelco. In 1968, a more representative year, employee accidents were the cause of nearly twice as much time off as strikes in Ontario.[25]

The former director of the United States Federal Mediation and Conciliation Service, William Simkin, remarked not long ago that the American record of time lost because of strikes "has been surprisingly good". One worker, on the average, loses one day by striking in every two or two-and-one-half years. "That, surely, is a small price to pay for freedom," Simkin commented. ". . . I rather facetiously say at times that if the Bureau of Labour Statistics could compile such a figure, they would discover that the effect of hangovers is more significant to the economy than the time lost through strikes."[26]

Like politicians supporting the flag or God or country, the anti-labour management messiahs frequently speak out against strikes in the public sector or in purportedly essential services. On these occasions, the business leaders exploit anti-labour feelings. Candour is neglected.

Behind these sanctimonious appeals for restrictions on strikes by civil employees, there is undoubtedly the feeling that the spokesmen's own industries, steel, mining, oil, should be classified as "essential" by some over-zealous government. The record shows little in industry that is truly "essential". It shows, too, that the impact of strikes has been enormously exaggerated. The 1969 International Nickel strike by some 17,000 Steelworkers dragged on for three months before ancillary plants scheduled their first lay-offs that were attributable to a short supply of the metal.

Many of the so-called labour "crises" in transportation and health "are fiction" says a U.S. industrial relations expert, Charles M. Rehmus.[27]

One of the few conclusions industrial relations students have come to over the years is that "essential-service" strikes and public-employee walkouts are much less disruptive and harmful than the public believes. In 1961 a U.S. Labour Department study of steel-industry strikes found "the economic impact of strikes on the economy is usually exaggerated. Too often the losses of production, employment and wages are evaluated in a context which assumes there would have been continuous high-level operation had there been no strike." In the U.S. coal industry, according to one writer, strikes have been positive forces, not emergencies, since historically they have diminished surpluses. Strikes, says this observer, have tended to "keep production in line with demand".[28]

Even in hospital strikes, the typical impact is not the death of scores of patients but a lessening of non-emergency admissions. Nowhere it seems can one find a report of a death at a hospital during a strike of orderlies or nurses.

What volunteers for the anti-labour crusade do not or choose not to understand is that an amount of uncertainty and an element of "emergency" are part of the bargaining process that helps both sides get to the settlement quickly. "The purpose of a strike threat is to create alarm," says the labour-relations theorist mentioned above. " . . . Once work has stopped, a main effort of each party is to give the impression that it has sufficient strength to carry on the strike indefinitely. . . . Publicity is almost always exaggerated. The actual detriment to the public welfare is only a fraction of that anticipated."[29]

Still, public opposition to strikes is encouraged by speakers from the upper-management class. It serves their purposes to distort, to confuse and to inflame public opinion on industrial relations. If the unions can be portrayed as selfish and inimical to the public interest, then union-busting, professional strike-breaking, industrial espionage and other anti-employee practices can be legitimized.

But more than just unionism is threatened in such an atmosphere of fear and suspicion. The history of repressive regimes throughout the world shows that employee associations are the first victims of autocracies. In Spain, Greece and other countries where militarist strong-arm governments have taken power, unions are typically emasculated or outlawed entirely.

Only a few important persons in Canadian labour relations have had the courage in recent years to speak out against the barking of the anti-union forces. Says Senator Carl Goldenberg, labour adviser to governments and a renowned mediator:

> The public must not be led to conclude from talk of strikes that union leaders are strikehappy. The facts are otherwise. . . . Strikes are, of course, the feature of labour-management relations which attracts most public attention. . . . Under a totalitarian regime, whether Fascist or Communist, there is an easy formula: strikes are prohibited.[30]

It would be prudent in the current debate over strikes and strikebreaking if the public heeded the words of a scholar in labour-management relations, Arvid Anderson, who says, "The only absolute guarantee against strikes is a police state."[31]

Notes

1. *Fortune, op. cit.,* p. 90.
2. Only one dairy was struck. Others locked out in support.
3. Mangold, William P., "On the Labour Front," *The New Republic,* October 3, 1934, p. 213.
4. Mitchell, Jonathon, "The Pinkertons Testify," *The New Republic,* March 31, 1937. The figure is based on investigations for the La Follette committee.
5. Levinson, Edward, *op cit.,* p. 724.
6. "Looking at the Labour Spy," *The New Republic,* October 7, 1938, p. 242.
7. La Follette, *op. cit.,* p. 135.
8. Levinson, *op. cit.,* p. 728.
9. Amidon, Beaulah, "Employers and the Spy Business," *Survey Graphic,* May 1, 1937, p. 266.
10. Nolan, Richard L., and Schneck, Rodney E., "Small Businessmen, Branch Managers, and Their Relative Susceptibility to Right-Wing Extremism: An Empirical Test," *Canadian Journal of Political Science,* March, 1969, p. 91.
11. *Ibid.,* p. 235.
12. Nolan and Schneck, *op. cit.,* p. 93.
13. *The Globe and Mail,* Report on Business, December 2, 1971.
14. *The* (Toronto) *Telegram,* August 26, 1969.
15. "Why Companies Take Tough Line on Unions," *Financial Post,* October 31, 1970.
16. "Is Collective Bargaining a Sick Institution?" *Canadian Transport,* November 15, 1970, p. 4.
17. Marting, Elizabeth (ed)., *Understanding Collective Bargaining,* American Management Association, Inc., New York, N.Y., 1959, p. 323.
18. *The Chatham News,* October 28, 1971.
19. Carrothers and Palmer, *op. cit.,* p. 255.
20. *Hansard,* October 7, 1970, p. 4684. The figures were supplied to Stephen Lewis, MPP for Scarborough-West, from labour board records surveyed by Martin Levinson, a prominent Toronto labour lawyer. Comparing the low number of votes won to the high percentages of automatic certifications, Lewis asked, ". . . Is it not interesting that this minister (Dalton Bales, the Minister of Labour) is prepared to give additional advantages to the vote system but to make it even harder to permit automatic certification?"
21. Carrothers and Palmer, *op. cit.,* p. 257.
22. *Hansard,* October 7, 1970, p. 4684.
23. *Financial Post,* January 2, 1971.
24. *The Globe and Mail,* June 25, 1970.

25. *The Maritime Co-operator*, Antigonish, N.S., March 1, 1969.
26. Law and Industrial Relations, Conference Proceedings, May 27, 1966, Centre for Industrial Relations, University of Toronto (not paginated).
27. "An Emergency at Sea," *Labour Law Journal*, October, 1963, p. 869.
28. Warren, Edgar, L., "Thirty-Six Years of National Emergency Strikes," *Industrial and Labour Relations Review*, University of California, Report No. 22, 1951, p. 11.
29. *Ibid.*, p. 15.
30. Paper presented in October, 1963, to the Fifth National Labour-Management Seminar, University of British Columbia.
31. Quoted in Polisar, Eric, "Strikes and Solutions," New York State School of Industrial and Labour Relations, Cornell University, 1968, p. 15.

3

How to Break a Strike

It's kind of like mobilizing an army, and once we've got our army together we send them to the place where the strike is going on. We usually send one guard for every fifteen men and we equip the guards with whatever weapons they need.[1]

Having Richard Grange break your strike means never having to do anything for yourself. Managements who engage Canadian Driver Pool literally hand over control of wide areas of their companies to Grange's lieutenants, far more control than any union contract would give the corporation's own employees. Grange's field marshals direct so much of the company's affairs during a strike that it is sometimes a wonder that the real owners ever gain control again once Grange has been paid off. Sometimes, he takes part of the company business with him, as in the case of Trane Company of Canada in Toronto. Trane engaged Canadian Driver Pool in 1971 for a strike by the United Electrical, Radio and Machine Workers of America. The strike having been settled with a new union contract, Grange walked out with a deal to take over cartage for Trane.

Grange not only recommends what a company should do to continue operating during a strike, he determines how many of his men the company will use. He will, if management wants, guarantee that the company will operate while its employees are on strike. He will recruit scabs. He will handle security. He will warehouse the company's products and guarantee that they are shipped to customers.

The company becomes a compound. A Driver Pool manual for employers says "every employee and member of the staff will be issued with a security button". Badges must be shown by anyone—visitors, too—leaving or entering the offices. The building is to be illuminated with floodlights, the manual directs. "This is very important." Not only are floodlights "important", they are intimidating, and probably intentionally so. The extensive strike preparations advised by Grange obviously cause more strikes than they prevent. A company turned suddenly into a fortress looks not only ready for war, but at war already. With a professional strikebreaker at his shoulder, the management negotiator has lost the incentive to bargain. In the eyes of the union negotiating committee, the struggle has already begun. They dig in. A strike becomes nearly inevitable.

Then Grange moves into strike action. More directives flow, all according to the book.

"Guards will accept parcels at the main entrance." Delivery-men will have to show identification. The licence plates of their vehicles are recorded.

Company supervisors are to be assigned to washrooms, the Grange manual for one employer dictates. Surveillance of the employees will be intensified during lunch hours "to stop any-one from spreading discontent or rumour in the washrooms, cafeteria or locker rooms". Supervisors are required by Grange to report "any incident, however small" and record each in "the incident book". Driver Pool will investigate. It says so in the manual.

Grange's scare tactics work well. When a management's telephone lines have been "swept" for non-existent taps, when floodlights are up, when Grange astonishes them with the exploits of his crew, the company executives are under his spell. He becomes their security adviser, a confidant of presidents, a Rasputin in the corporate castle. If he tells them they need a new alarm system, he can recommend one: his own. In 1972 he bought a franchise for Ontario to sell burglar alarms under the name Provincial Security Systems Limited.

Communications are handled in army-fashion, too. Grange, the ersatz commander, directs the operations through a booming radio signal piped from his base station's 60-foot antenna atop an apartment building at 2240 Weston Road in the north-western section of Metropolitan Toronto. In Apartment 1803 is a branch office of Driver Pool, where the photographic achievements of Grange's men are developed.

Station wagons rented to his clients from another Grange subsidiary, Metro Car Lease, are equipped with two-way radios that link Grange's human satellites to one of the most powerful radio networks—legal or underground—anywhere in the province. According to the federal Transport Department, neither Grange nor any one of his various companies and fronts has a citizens' band licence required by law to operate the antenna and equipment at his radio station.

Inside the company, now almost a heavily-secured fort, a Grange trooper co-ordinates manoeuvres. In the heyday of American strikebreaking, before various U.S. states broke up professional strikebreaking gangs, the inside men were called "nobles" in the argot of the profession.

A former strikebreaker years ago made a public confession, a testimonial to himself, really, in which he described the "noble."

A noble, as the word implies, is a swanky aristocrat, a care-free, swaggering knight of America's roaming nobility, who at times risks the smoothness of his skin in miniature battles with aggressive strikers while playing the game of protecting property and strikebreaking during the active labour erup-tions.[2]

Describing one typical noble, the author, an "old-time fink", said the noble "knew no fear". Paradoxically, the noble loved it. "A gang of jeering strikers was to him what a red flag is to a bull."[3]

The description fits the Grange operation, because appear-ances are crucial to the strikebreaking profession's success. The struck plant, once Grange is done modifying it to the status of a bivouacked army under seige, must appear to be threatened.

Grange makes company employees park their cars in the centre of the company lot, away from fences, sidewalks and driveways. The image of covered wagons huddling nervously is appropriate.

Driver Pool's manual explains why: ". . . to prevent damage from bottles of acid etc., being tossed over the compound fence." Grange has worked more than 30 strikes since 1969, and in not one has a bottle of acid been thrown.

There are obvious reasons why Grange and other professional strikebreaking agencies intimidate their own clients and the company's employees. If photographing the strikers, running trucks (sometimes empty) across their picket lines, or other tactics are successful in causing a disturbance, then more strikeguards will be necessary. Driver Pool and other successful professional strikebreaking concerns create their own markets. Says Greg Ross, another one-time Grange employee, "The company's not going to pay for anything if there's nothing happening."

Professional strikebreakers will do more than just hope for trouble. Trouble is their business, and they know how to make it. During a 1971 strike by the International Chemical Workers' Union at Canadian Johns-Manville in Port Union, Ontario, outside Metro Toronto, the president of the local union says he received telephone calls from men who he knows worked for Driver Pool who challenged him to fight. The strike was one of Grange's worst for violent episodes, which create the best conditions for Driver Pool.

Six strikers, according to a former Driver Pool employee, were beaten up during the lengthy strike. Driver Pool guards armed with guns and nightsticks patrolled the expansive grounds of the company. When there was no action, says one strikebreaker, Grange's toughs would chase rabbits through the long fields around the Manville complex in Driver Pool's rented automobiles.

At Gidon Industries in northwest Metro Toronto, a Grange "noble" was charged with assault on two occasions, once when a union supporter was thrown from the plant after being fired. The second charge followed a chase inside the plant after another union sympathizer was accused of loafing and dismissed.

In early 1972 at Central Precision Limited, a suburban Toronto company that rebuilds car engines, the local union president's car was firebombed, and a gang of Driver Pool's toughs, identified from photographs by the strikers, attacked a trailer used for a strike headquarters.

During another strike, according to Driver Pool sources, strikebreakers smashed the windshield of a car they were using but told Grange that the strikers had done it.

Grange builds his own image by romanticizing the work of his strikebreakers. Readers of an American magazine, in a story by sometime *Toronto Star* writer Alan Edmonds, saw this embroidered version, in Grange's own words, of how Driver Pool personnel moved a shipment of liquid sugar from Redpath Sugars Limited during a 1971 strike:

"We spent hours going over the plans of the plant and we set things up for a 60-second exposure at the picket line. First, three support cars swept up to the gate to get it open. It took them 30 seconds. Two photographers were dropped at the gate and started shooting pictures while the cars went on to the front of the building.

"The trucks were all warmed up, ready to go. So one car drops the driver and his crew, who get into the cab and start moving. Another car sweeps out ahead, then comes the truck, and the last car picks up the photographers at the gate.

"We have another car at the rear of the picket line getting pictures of the strikers in case any of them pick up rocks to heave at the truck.

"The truck is going to hit a stop light, we know that. We also know the picketers are going to get in their cars and follow it. So we have pictures taken of the licence plates of the strikers' cars, and then our cars close in behind the truck at the stop light. When it goes green the truck moves off and our cars block the road to the strikers. And the truck gets clean away. It was a very sweet operation."[4]

Grange got at least $75,000 from Redpath, according to Donald Whitteker, the company sales manager who was the principal contact with Driver Pool during the strike.[5]

There was one side to the trucking adventure that Edmonds and Grange did not point out, however. Grange's driver-crews— typical of professional strikebreaking operations—are so untroubled by the presence of picket lines they tend not to stop at all.

In at least seven strikes Grange has been involved in, drivers have either hit strikers or missed them so narrowly that charges were laid.[6] Three Grange employees have been convicted of reckless or dangerous driving, have been fined or have lost their driver's licences for running down or nearly hitting strikers. A Driver Pool strikebreaker who lost his licence before he ran down a picketing worker got a new licence using the address of the Napoli Meat Market at 7250 Hutchison in Montreal and a phoney name. Charges were pending against two other Driver Pool heavies in May, 1972, for picket line incidents with cars. Grange's own driving record at the provincial Department of Transportation showed in June, 1972, that he had no driver's licence. Driver Pool regular John Vance's driving record shows his licence has been pulled, and he is listed as "unrenewable". Vance's driving record includes convictions for driving with defective brakes, speeding 40 miles over the legal maximum, dangerous driving and driving without a licence—a total of 27 convictions from January, 1967, to December, 1971.

In the 1972 strike at Union Carbide's Oakville oxygen facility, a local Justice of the Peace refused to accept an information for a complaint from Fred Geddes, an official of the Oil, Chemical and Atomic Workers' International Union, against a Driver Pool man who was driving a car that rammed Geddes's after racing past the picket line. The J.P. claimed Geddes wouldn't be able to prove the charge. His insurance campany, says Geddes, states that exactly $100 damage was done to his car.

In Brantford, Ontario, during the lengthy Texpack Limited strike in 1971, charges were laid against the driver of a scabs' bus and a truck driver. The trucker, said police, swerved his vehicle into the path of a line of women strikers. The same driver was involved in a picket-line accident outside AP Parts Canada Limited in suburban Toronto, where the little-known Extra Driver Services supplied drivers and trucks during a United Auto Workers' strike in 1971. Grange tells potential clients to call AP Parts for a reference.

Luckily, so far, no Ontario unionists have been recorded as fatalities under the wheels of strikebreaker-driven trucks. But James Gordon Harvey, an employee of Shell Canada Limited near Burnaby, British Columbia, was run over and killed during a 1969 strike by the Oil, Chemical and Atomic Workers' International Union. "Harvey's death," said Ray Haynes, secretary-treasurer of the B.C. Federation of Labour, "can be directly attributed to the importation of strikebreakers."[7]

How Driver Pool hustlers behind the wheel feel about their jobs is evident from the testimony of a former strikebreaker, David B. Davies, who appeared at the preliminary hearing in 1971 in Grange's trial for illegal conspiracy to wiretap a union office.

Davies told the court that a Driver Pool trucker usually has another partner in the cab. "I guess just like the old stagecoach," said Davies, "they'd be called 'shotgun'."[8]

Grange's propensity for embellishing the driving exploits of his strikebreakers, such as the use of empty air tanks on their trucks, conceals the truth that such driving practices are unsafe. A truck with its braking apparatus partially dismantled is a potential wrecking machine on wheels.

For someone who has never been on strike, it is almost impossible to imagine the anxiety created by the presence of professional strikebreakers. Strikers themselves are often unable to articulate it. It would be untrue to say that there has never been a violent act committed in desperation by a picketer. It would be equally implausible to expect even an ardent pacifist to stand aside while an intruder was stealing from a victim's home. When what is stolen is a job, a livelihood and a means of support perhaps for a whole family, the angry reactions of strikers should hardly be surprising.

Ed Morrison watched Driver Pool try to break a strike in late 1971 and early 1972 at National Sewer Pipe Limited in Clarkson, Ontario. "It makes the fellas up-tight," says Morrison, a long-time employee and secretary of Local 239 of the United Glass and Ceramic Workers of America. "They see someone taking their bread and butter." Three strikers were arrested and charged with causing damages during the strike. Each was fined $100.

What is so frustrating to men like Ed Morrison is that Driver Pool and other professional strikebreakers protract a strike, make windfalls and then leave as the union and management make virtually the same deal that each could have found acceptable when the strike was still young.

Grange, in three years of strikebreaking, has actually been involved only once in successful union-busting. That was in late 1970 when he was called on to supply drivers for W. J. Mowat Cartage Limited. An independent union, not the International Brotherhood of Teamsters, walked out to protest the firing of a popular driver. (The man had been accused of negligence for disabling a truck's engine. Nearly 200 other drivers went out on strike in sympathy for his reinstatement.)

In job after job, Grange and professional strikebreakers like him have walked away with handsome profits while only delaying an eventual settlement that in the majority of cases was better (from the union position) than the company's last pre-strike offer. At AP Parts, for instance, the settlement after the six-week strike in 1971 was worth 89 cents an hour, compared with 79 offered before the strike. At National Sewer Pipe Company, recalls Ed Morrison, "They told us"—before the strike—"here's 18 cents, take it or leave it." The final setttlement was worth 45 cents an hour.

At Johns-Manville, the company's pre-strike offer totalled 39 cents an hour for a three-year contract. Robert Stewart, an official of the International Chemical Workers, says the final agreement provided 56 cents and a cost-of-living bonus arrangement not in the pre-strike offer. The more critical issue in the Johns-Manville strike, however, appeared to be safety conditions. The company makes asbestos products. A dozen employees of the Manville plant have died of cancer or the lung disease asbestosis in just the past couple of years, says Stewart. Even the families of the employees exposed to asbestos are not safe. The toxic fibres are carried out of the plant in clothing and in the hair. Johns-Manville budged only a little on the safety issue, although safety is an issue in all the multi-national corporation's plants. The entire city of Manville in New Jersey, site of another Johns-Manville asbestos operation, faces a disastrous health problem. In 1972 the mortality rate due to asbestosis encountered in the atmosphere was expected to reach 200 to 500 deaths above normal.[9] In the one year since the Port Union, Ontario, strike when the company used Driver Pool, three more workers in the Johns-Manville plant have died, says Stewart. The company paid Grange $30,000 for his work, according to a former associate.

A big contradiction that stands out in the professional strikebreaking racket is the money paid strikebreakers while the client company insists it cannot meet union contract proposals. Thus, truck drivers paid $3 or $4 an hour watch as their jobs are manned by industrial mercenaries for whom Grange gets $7.75 an hour. A photographer costs $10 an hour.

Company executives declare that in Grange's first sales talk, it sounds incredible that he can offer so much and the potential of union-free management for so little. Some don't realize at the time that Grange will assign 10 men for 10 hours a day and invoice the company for $700 a day. On top of that will be truck-rental bills, camera expenses and of course, the dogs ($2.50 an hour and up). For extra protection, Grange recommends that spies be sent into a plant up to one month before a strike could legally start. Assuming there's a union left, he counsels, spies should be kept around after the strike, to check up on agitators.

Grange gets the money, but all his personnel appear on the payrolls of companies that use Driver Pool. This makes it easier to conceal spies on the union and helps evade the laws against unlicenced transport companies and unlicenced security guards. If Transport Department investigators show up, Grange's clients could claim his drivers as their own employees.

Grange is an advocate of the four-day week. For his clients, not his own employees. "This arrangement," says a Driver Pool manual, "will lessen the exposure of the employees to picketing." The short week doesn't undercut his own profits, though. The new Grange work day will be 10 hours for companies that take his advice. In some 30 strikes none has.

Grange is not nearly so generous with his own employees. He lets them work themselves to exhaustion. They make big salaries—$400 gross weekly paycheques are common, according to a former bookkeeper—but they work 80 hours a week and longer to do it.

While drivers work 12, 14 and 16 hours a day hauling for

Grange's clients, his strikeguards have comfy jobs, sitting in parked cars, taking pictures and radioing their boss for directives. It is another contradiction that unionists can't understand: how managements can fight alleged "featherbedding" practices and job-security rules proposed by union negotiating committees while paying Grange's loafers to sit around and take pictures at $7 to $10 an hour. Inside the plant, Driver Pool nobles pose as company executives and do even less.

Doing nothing is an old-time habit in strikebreaking circles. Two American authors who studied the business commented, "The job of the professional strikebreaker was to smash picket lines, to give the appearance that the plant was operating, and to incite violence so that public authorities would take action against the unionists."[10] As strikebreaker "jobs" they list driving empty trucks through picket lines and burning paper in the company furnaces so that emissions from the smokestacks would give the appearance of production going on. Generally, then and now, what the professional strikebreaker does inside the corporate offices is "merely amuse himself in the plant to while away the time".[11] The professional strikebreakers don't work in the plant. They become, like Driver Pool salesman Irving Geller, a high-fashion-attired one time mutual-fund pusher and teacher, a quasi-executive. At a Steelworkers' strike at the Toronto plant of Macotta Company of Canada Limited in 1972, Geller, a one-time U.S. Marine, ejected a reporter from the plant and ordered a company officer whom the reporter was interviewing to say nothing to the press.[12]

For help and advice like this, Macotta, Gidon Industries (another plant run by Geller until he was kicked out after getting into too many fights with employees) and other companies gladly pay Driver Pool sums like $4,000 a week (in Gidon's case).

Strikeguards like Grange's and the assortment of shock troops and other strike supervisors supplied by Grange are different from ordinary scabs, who cross the picket lines to take the strikers' jobs. While the scab wants to work, the professional strikebreaker doesn't want anybody's job.

One of Grange's ex-strikebreakers, Al Rusnell, says everyone understood perfectly what Driver Pool's role was in a strike. He was a cameraman for a time.

"We were there to aggravate people," he says. Rusnell thought Grange's Cart-Rite Cartage would be a legitimate trucking company, not a strikebreaking arm. He got out in early 1971 to set up his own trucking company.

The overpaid lieutenants, who loafed, and the drivers, who hauled long hours, were bound to clash. Even the drugs freely passed around Grange's warehouse couldn't prevent tension in the organization.

For a time in 1971 the Grange operation was in turmoil, even before the leader and a moonlighting Metropolitan Toronto policeman were arrested on wiretap charges.

First Grange's father, Alfred, the retired Canadian Imperial Bank of Commerce executive, declined to do the bookkeeping anymore for his son's conglomeration of trucking, leasing, warehousing and security companies.

Then the men who had been the backbone of the trucking side of the operations began taking off. "I figured somebody's going to get hurt, and it wasn't going to be me," says Al Rusnell. Craig Symons, once Grange's partner in Cart-Rite, deserted him. "I didn't like looking over my shoulder all the time on the way home," Symons tells friends. Barry Dantzic, a former policeman and son of a respected and popular Toronto policeman, also quit. The younger Dantzic had been a partner in Cart-Rite. David Davies, another original partner in Cart-Rite, also left, to go to university. They all agree it was Grange's decision to concentrate on strike work and to recruit extensively from an underworld of ex-convicts and social misfits that drove them from the organization. All had been long-time friends of Grange. Earlier, the outfit's original lawyer, Archibald Greenaway, dropped the organization's business.

The drivers were so upset, one called the provincial Labour Department's employment standards branch. An investigator, Klaus Wehrenberg, looked into a complaint that in shifting drivers and heavies from Cart-Rite to Driver Pool, Grange had been double payrolling to evade the laws on wage exploitation, vacation pay and hours of work. Although the 48-hour week is the legal limit (without a Labour Department permit to go another eight hours), Grange got away with scheduling men for 60, 80 and 100 hours a week, according to ex-employees, by paying them part of their wages with Cart-Rite cheques, part with Canadian Driver Pool.

The Labour Department did nothing, however, although one former strikebreaker remembers Wehrenberg told him that the investigator wanted to continue his probe, but that higher officials in the department wouldn't let him.

The mistrust and dissension among Grange's troops—he had up to 75 men on his payrolls at one time in 1971—nearly erupted. Money and the promise of bigger purses kept the men quiet.

Grange and one of his veteran strikebusters, Peter Paynter, almost broke up during 1971. Paynter (he also uses the first name Pieter, and his driver's licence is in the name Christopher Paynter) was ambitious and wanted to lead Driver Pool "in the field" as he called it. He called himself in self-deprecation a "van boy" and hated the cartage work. Like many in the organization, probably, he felt he was executive material.

Paynter worried that Grange was going to fire him. When strike business was low, Grange's drivers would be laid off according to a seniority system. "Last in, first out," he would say. Paynter had been picked up by Immigration Department officials in the United States while driving a truck of oil barrels during a strike by the Oil, Chemical and Atomic Workers' International Union at the Toronto operation of Veedol Oil. Paynter was deported to his home in England when he could not prove that he had an immigrant's work permit in either the U.S. or Canada. He called Grange—collect—but Grange refused to accept the charges. Paynter returned anyway, but found himself a low man. Paynter, say ex-drivers, lived for a time in the Pool warehouse to avoid detection by immigration officials. On June 23, 1972, Paynter was ordered deported after a hearing in Toronto before Immigration Department officials, who charged he had entered the country and worked illegally. The deportation order was to take effect after Paynter faced criminal charges pending against him. He is appealing the deportation ruling. Paynter has now risen again in Driver Pool platoons, doing guard work, driving scabs, and handling dogs. But before his status soared again he was to write in his diary, "I wish I had the money to tell them where to shove their job." He does not appear to have reached his goal of field commander in the organization.

To a man like Paynter, a man who lived with one of Grange's Dobermans and who toys with guns, the Canadian Driver Pool operation is fun and profitable. Grange runs it like a secret police. An instruction book for new recruits says anyone brought into the band must be sponsored by a present member. After a two-month initiation period, working on trial with his sponsor, the new recruit will be voted on by present employees.

Grange instructs his agents never to reveal whom they really work for. They are to say they are employed by the company whose strike the are trying to break. Cameras are not to be used for personal use. Licence-plate numbers of strikers' cars should be photographed. On the strike scene, Driver Pool guards and drivers are required to fill in detailed forms that ask whom they photographed, what licence plates they observed and what "incidents" occurred. Off-duty behaviour should be guarded so that the employee isn't an embarrassment to Driver Pool. Carrying weapons on a job will mean instant dismissal. Finally, don't get involved in fighting. The last two rules are enforced loosely.

At a strike at Union Carbide in 1972, a Driver Pool man was charged with possession of a dangerous weapon, a crow-bar. "All of us carried a four-way wheel wrench," recalls one strikebreaker who has left Driver Pool. "I don't think anybody ever crossed the picket line without some kind of weapon." The tire-chain is another popular tool of the trade. The driver of a scabs' bus during the 1971 Texpack strike in Brantford, Johannes Venhorst, carried one at his side.[13] And so did Howie Gardner, who worked as a scab garbage loader in Ottawa in the summer of 1971 during a strike by employees of Ottawa Disposal Systems Limited. Of course, said Gardner, it was only for protection. "I don't think I'll ever have to use it. It should discourage them from getting too close."[14]

Grange's men occasionally feel exploited, enough so to complain to the Department of Labour. But they make hundreds of dollars a week. Other scabs don't fare as well. What the professional strikebreaker and the casual scab have in common is that both are contract labour.

In Ontario the worker sent to a job on contract labour through a hiring agency has no protection under the Employment Standards Act against cheating on the minimum wage or other basic conditions set down by law. They pay their own pension contributions, their own income tax, travel expenses and medical insurance premiums. In any large city there are contract-labour shops that readily refer the unemployed to strikes, sometimes without telling the worker he or she is expected to scab. In several states in the U.S., employment agencies must tell their applicants that a strike is in progress. Not in Ontario.

Toronto has many labour contractors. Irvine H. Williams, who claims he introduced the practice to Canada, calls them "labour slave markets". They take as much as 50 per cent of the paycheque from people they "give" jobs to, often leaving the unskilled or semi-skilled scab with less than the minimum wage, says Williams.

In Toronto and other cities in Ontario there is Office Overload; Laborquest and Handy Andy Labour Service are others.

Williams, a former partner in Employers Overload Company, says "practically any slave market will send people to a plant on strike if the police will protect them". Laborquest pays drivers $2.25 an hour, everyone else $1.65, the provincial minimum wage, according to a source in the employment field.

Management typically pays "much more, always" for scab labour than it pays its own employees because the reason for using scabs is to break the strike at any cost, not to produce, says Williams. One common formula in the "slave markets", says Williams, is to charge management one-third above the hourly rate that prevailed before the strike.

When he was still in the business (he is semi-retired), Williams would get six or seven calls a week from personnel executives who wanted scab labour. "Sometimes I got involved," says Williams, "sometimes I didn't." He says he was detached from the issues of the strike. "Guys would come back to tell me, 'That company you sent me to is on strike.' That's the first I heard of it." He claims he could supply 200 workers at a time. "I'm ashamed I started the whole business," he says now.

Nothing in the Employment Agencies Act of Ontario bars an agency from recruiting scabs. Several state governments in the United States have curbed the use of private employment agencies as strikebreaker hiring-halls. At least five states categorically prohibit employment agencies or any company not involved in the dispute from hiring scabs. New York City, the country's biggest megalopolis, has it own statute outlawing involvement of employment agencies in strikes. The states with such legislation are Pennsylvania, Washington, New Jersey, Hawaii and Delaware. Typically the laws provide penalties of up to a $1,000 fine and a year in jail.

Immigrants are regular victims of the "labour slave market". Often underskilled and desperate for work some will understandably take any work, even when it takes them across the picket lines of other recent immigrants. They are numerous, and they work cheaply.

Many industrial ghetto plants actively recruit immigrants. In a strike involving Greeks, Italians and Portuguese at Allanson Manufacturing Company of Toronto in 1969, president Roy A. Crolly admitted to a newspaperman that his striking employees were "primarily unskilled, so it's easy to replace them". He did, and broke the United Steelworkers of America strike after three months. Starting rates were $1.50 an hour for men, $1.40 for women.

"The companies exploit Pakistanis and Negroes, people who have tremendous problems about normal employment," declares Ross Russell, director of organization for the United Electrical, Radio and Machine Workers of America. "They do the dirtiest, hardest manual labour."

An immigrant from Trinidad only five months, Russell Hinds, applied for work at Gidon Industries after seeing the company's advertisement in the *Toronto Star*. (It is also illegal in many American states for companies in labour disputes to withhold that fact from help-wanted advertisements. But not in Canada.) Hinds says a Gidon supervisor, Robert Kettle, told him he could have a job (this was before the Steelworkers' strike began on March 27, 1972), "providing you don't join the union".

Hinds, an experienced welder in Trinidad, complained that there were not enough safety goggles for everyone welding on Gidon's muffler assembly lines. He hurt his hands shoving fibreglass tubes into muffler frames. A foreman told him to run them under cold water. He attended a beer-and-chicken party thrown by the company shortly before the strike. "It seemed to me," says Hinds, "it was to get people on the company side. They might feel if you don't go, well, you don't like the company." He signed up with the Steelworkers before the strike and was fired.

Many immigrants work while not legally entitled to, since they entered Canada on visitors' permits and are not landed immigrants. Some two dozen illegal immigrants were kicked out of Gidon, where Canadian Driver Pool had helped recruit them and brought them through picket lines in station wagons rented by the company from Grange. Manpower and Immigration Department investigators, acting on a complaint from the union, found the immigrants and chased them out.

At another strike protracted by Driver Pool, illegal Portuguese immigrants were discovered by immigration authorities at Pre-Con Limited, a pre-cast concrete manufacturer in Brampton, Ontario. The response from the company was typical when Ray Ford, an official of Local 506 of the Labourers' International Union of North America, charged that "at least 75 per cent" of 125 scabs were in the country illegally. "We have quite a number of Portuguese people working for us," said the company's negotiator, Ronald Bradley, "and whether they're legal or not, we don't know." (Immigration law says that employers who lure illegal immigrants into Canada to work could be fined up to $500 and be sentenced to six months in jail.) Bradley, a former conciliation officer for the provincial Labour

Department, said that if scabs he had hired were unlawful immigrants, ". . . it isn't our responsibility to find out".[15]

While Europeans and West Indians are popular for employers who use low-paid strikebreakers, American scabs are more skilled and are paid accordingly. Just before an expected strike of airport fueling personnel in 1967, their American-owned employer, Consolidated Aviation Fueling of Toronto Limited, imported 15 American supervisors to break the strike. The Minister of Manpower and Immigration at the time, Jean Marchand, ordered them out of the country within 48 hours. The scabs had not informed border authorities that they intended to work.[16]

In the 1964 Toronto newspaper strike, at least 15 professional strikebreakers were brought in from the United States, according to the International Typographical Union. ITU officers told the story to the Royal Commission Inquiry into Labour Disputes headed by Justice Ivan Rand. The strikebreakers were paid $1,035 a week and an extra $15 a day in expenses, said ITU representatives Allan Histed and Allan Heritage.[17]

During a strike in 1969 by the Textile Workers' Union of America, 16 "fixers" were imported by Hanes Hosiery Limited in Toronto from a North Carolina plant of its U.S.-owned parent to keep the machinery from breaking down. (In both the Pre-Con and Hanes strikes, the Ontario Labour Relations Board, on the basis of the companies' conduct, granted consent to the striking unions to prosecute the companies in court for breaking the Labour Relations Act's requirements to bargain in good faith.) Strikeguards supplied by Anning Investigations Limited helped escort the American scabs through the picket lines at Hanes. MPP Stephen Lewis of the New Democratic Party said later that year in the Legislature, "It is apparently perfectly permissible to come into this country on a visitor's pass with a work permit for the purpose of strikebreaking."[18]

Like so many other American-owned companies in Canada, Hanes was acting out a familiar pattern in American labour relations in the minority of states where no restrictions on strikebreaking exist. In 1958 Hanes had defeated a strike and kicked out the Textile Union. Seven years later the Textile Workers got a campaign going, and eight union sympathizers were fired. The National Labour Relations Board ordered all of them reinstated and made Hanes pay $46,000 in back pay with six per cent interest.[19]

Mechanical strikebreakers, not only human ones, are similarly immune from government interference in Canada. Trucks from the United States are licenced to run scab-made products back to the U.S. from Canadian subsidiaries and other companies without interference from the provincial Transport Department.

However, Richard Grange's companies have been charged a number of times for violations of the Public Commercial Vehicles Act. In one case that came to trial in 1971, Intercontinental Container Leasing Limited, the company Grange set up to rent trailers to himself and his clients, was fined $50 for operating without a public commercial-vehicle licence. But Grange and the strikebreaking business keep on rolling along.

Notes

1. Basso, Hamilton, "Strike-Buster: Man Among Men," *The New Republic*, December 12, 1934, p. 125.
2. "By an Old-Time Fink," "Nobles and Finks," *Saturday Evening Post*, April 11, 1925, p. 12.
3. *Ibid.*
4. "Strike-breaking Inc.," *The Capitalist Reporter,* January, 1972, p. 10.
5. *Her Majesty the Queen vs. Barry Chapman and Richard Grange*, Provincial Court (Criminal Division), County of York, (Trial transcript) p. 308.
6. Smith & Stone, Georgetown, Ont. (1970); Redpath Sugars Ltd., Toronto (1971); W. J. Mowat Cartage Ltd., Toronto (1970); Gidon Industries Ltd., Toronto (1971); Union Carbide Canada Ltd., Oakville, Ont. (1970); AP Parts, Toronto (1971); Canadian Phoenix Steel & Pipe, Toronto (1971).
7. *The* (Toronto) *Telegram*, August 27, 1969.
8. *Her Majesty the Queen vs. Barry Chapman and Richard Grange*, Provincial Court (Criminal Division), County of York (Preliminary hearing transcript), p. 110.
9. "Asbestos Cited as Cause of Cancer Epidemic," *Textile Labour,* Publication of the Textile Workers' Union of America, May, 1972, p. 17.
10. Taylor and Witney, *op. cit.*, p. 125.
11. *Ibid.*
12. *The Globe and Mail*, April 8, 1972, p. 5.
13. *The Brantford Expositor*, Sept. 4, 1971, p. 1.
14. *The Ottawa Citizen*, August 12, 1971, p. 37.
15. *The* (Toronto) *Telegram*, August 14, 1970.
16. *The Globe and Mail*, October 5, 1967.
17. *The Globe and Mail*, May 10, 1967, p. B2.
18. Pamphlet published by the New Democratic Party of Ontario based on *Hansard*, p. 13.
19. *Ibid.*, p. 10.

4

Who Is Richard Grange, and Why Is He (with all his friends) Breaking So Many Strikes?

"There's more money in industry than there ever was in crime."

R. J. Coach,
"Cleveland's most famous strikebreaking chief"[1]

Strikebreaking is practically the only business anyone can get into without a breath of experience in any legitimate enterprise. It takes no special training, no education and hardly any motive other than to covet power and money.

The strikebreaking racket has always attracted ex-convicts and thugs. Many American authorities have realized that untrained and unstable men who adore strong-man tactics and violence are dangerous individually but more so in strikebreaking mobs, and put them out of business long ago. Canadian governments, however, have tolerated the practice and indeed, it may be said, have fostered its growth by considerately looking the other way while professional strikebreakers infiltrate legitimate businesses, deny employees their lawful rights and poison industrial relations.

The professional strikebreakers appearing at picket lines and working undercover in industries in Ontario today fit a pattern well documented by the strikebreaking investigations of the U.S. Senate Committee on Education and Labour in the late 1930's (the La Follette committee). "Men available for strike work" from strikeguard agencies, declared the committee in one of its most revealing reports, "are generally socially maladjusted . . . they constitute a sort of underworld, and many of them have criminal records or are professional criminals."[2]

An official of one strikebreaking company told about the kind of operatives used by professional strikebreakers. " . . . There is always something wrong with most of them," he said, "or they wouldn't be in that business."[3] Senator Robert M. La Follette Jr.'s committee compiled a list of every strikebreaker known. The La Follette report said, "That approximately one-third of the strikebreakers listed should be discovered . . . to have criminal or arrest records shows how closely the strikebreaking business approaches a gangland racket."[4] The estimates of the number of ex-convicts employed by professional strikebreakers often ranged much higher.

Untrained, possibly armed, many with violent histories, the professional strikebreakers in Ontario today would be a potential threat to the public even if they were only meeting informally and not directing most of their activity against the union movement. In tension-ridden situations, like those at picket lines, where hostility is inspired by the strikebreaker's own presence, behind the wheel of a scabs' bus or a two-ton trailer-truck rig, the typical strikebreaker is a volatile time bomb. Yet police departments in many communities in Ontario where professional strikebreakers have appeared have helped them do their work. And government officials have taken a dangerously lackadaisical attitude towards the presence of strikebreaking gangs in their communities.

Things may have changed since 1913, when the leader of a strikebreaking gang testified at a U.S. commission on industrial relations that one of the first requirements for his guards "was shooting ability". But not much. A Canadian Driver Pool tough at the Redpath Sugars Limited strike in 1971 pointed a gun at several strikers. Even the safety of other drivers is in peril when some Driver Pool men—"doped to the bloody eyeballs," as one ex-strikebreaker remembers them—barrel down the highway.

Driver Pool includes a corps of men whose backgrounds are as diverse as they are typical of the professional strikebreaking business in North America. Police files and former employees reveal that the exploits of some Driver Pool personnel have included theft, armed robbery, counterfeiting, stealing cars, breaking-and-entering, cheque forging, conspiracy, assault, wiretapping, driving under the influence of drugs, bombing, gun

57

smuggling, hit-and-run, prostitution, arson and connections with reputed members of the organized crime world commonly called the Mafia.

Based on the American experience, it should surprise no one that similar "types" congregate in the strikebreaking business in Ontario today. Of the 40 key men employed most regularly by Canadian Driver Pool, more than half have arrest or criminal records or are well-known to the police, according to former employees and police officials. Such a gang would not be allowed to meet openly and work in highly visible jobs without a public outcry and almost constant police surveillance unless they were operating a strikebreaking business. Only in an anti-union climate is a brigade like Canadian Driver Pool allowed to function legally. They are hired for intimidation by companies, ostensibly to protect property, though nothing in the performance of Driver Pool or security guard forces acting as strikebreakers shows they have succeeded in perpetrating anything but ill-feeling, provocative tension and mistrust.

Some unionists find it incredible that major corporations like Imperial Oil, Dominion Glass, Duplate, Kimberly-Clark, Kraftco, Getty Oil, Johns-Manville and their subsidiaries would get near professional strikebreakers like these. Some corporations even conceal their complicity. United Auto Workers negotiator Pat Smith recalls telling Honeywell Controls management after signing a new contract in 1972, "Well, you won't have to use Richard Grange this time." Smith says the company's chief negotiator, Douglas Montrose, said, "What are you talking about?" A front for Driver Pool called Canadian Specialized Security Limited was standing by the night the Honeywell workers voted to accept the negotiated contract, according to a former strikebreaker. Specialized Security was set up when Grange personally couldn't get a provincial licence to run a security agency. Honeywell had used Driver Pool in 1970. The connection was made through Grange's wife, Marilyn, whose father is a Honeywell executive.

The face Richard Allen Grange, 28-year-old strikebreaker, shows to the public is but a silhouette that conceals more about him than he would like you to know. He could have had an average upper-middle-class youth, much the same as any other adopted son of a bank official. In the late 1950's, when Rick was maturing, the Grange family lived in one of Toronto's best neighbourhoods, the Leaside area. He ran with a gang of bored but well-to-do teen-aged friends in the early 1960's.

Rick Grange's cronies were all like him, irrepressible, to say the least. But not all of them had been convicted on 12 charges of breaking and entering and theft, in connection with burglaries at a neighbourhood shopping plaza. Grange was lucky, however, and he got a suspended sentence (in January, 1963). He was 17. When Grange was in court after his 1972 conviction on charges of conspiracy to wiretap a union office, lawyer G. Arthur Martin described his client's record as a "youthful escapade".

Having graduated at last from Northern Vocational School, Grange, now in his early 20's, picked up other interests. He enrolled in the Ontario College of Art, a provincially-financed school for painting, sculpture and design near downtown Toronto. His specialty was pen-and-ink sketches. "I am an artist," Grange bragged in 1971 to a newspaper. ". . . All my life I have painted. I created. I'm an industrial designer by profession. I look at business as a theory of art. When you are building a business you are creating for yourself, and for your employees."[5] The brainwashing worked, and soon reporters were writing up the prep-school-faced strikebreaker who "is apparently 27 years old, a university graduate and a Canadian. . . ."[6] In fact he went to O.C.A. for only a few weeks in late 1967 and left in January, 1968. College officials say he quit "for personal reasons". He hadn't stayed long enough to get any marks. For a time he worked in a gas station.

In 1968 Grange and old friends from Leaside went into business for themselves. They repaired cars in a garage near Eglinton Avenue and Mount Pleasant Road in Toronto near a principally residential area in the north-central part of the city. For most of them, in particular Grange, it was an amazingly lucrative business. Friends recall he would run up a $1,300 bill in one night at Granny's, his favourite nightclub. "He bragged like crazy about how much money he was making," one friend recollects. Grange claims he made fabulous sums playing the stock market.

On Hallowe'en night in 1968 Metro Toronto Police auto-squad detectives raided the garage and found a 1966 black Corvette coupe stolen 10 months earlier in Williamsville, New York.

Four of Grange's friends were arrested five weeks later and charged: 24-year-old Neil McClelland, David B. Davies, 26, Robert Edward "Ted" LaPalm, 24, and Paul Chisholm, 23. Auto-squad investigators pieced together the Toronto half of a ring, they said, that stole only luxury cars like Cadillacs, Corvettes and Porsches.

The cars were stolen in Buffalo and other parts of New York and sold to car dealers in Toronto and to private customers in southern Ontario, Montreal and other places as far away as Whitehorse in the Yukon.[7] Within days of the raid the police had found 22 cars and expected to locate 20 others. They never did. The cars had been sold for $3,000, $4,000 and $5,000 and were worth $5,000 to $7,000 each.[8]

All four who were charged were convicted May 1, 1970, and served prison sentences of up to nine months for their role in the ring. A fifth man was charged originally, but the charges were dropped. On the American side, no arrests were made.

The car-ring episode resurfaced after Grange's arrest with Metro Toronto policeman Barry Chapman on charges of conspiracy to wiretap a union office during the 1971 strike at Redpath Sugars Limited. David B. Davies returned to testify against Grange at the trial. Davies had worked for Cart-Rite Cartage and Canadian Driver Pool after getting out of jail, sometimes as a driver, other times as a $175-a-week cameraman.

While Grange's friends were awaiting their trial, Grange got the idea for Cart-Rite Cartage. He and a friend, Bob Greenaway (Greenaway's father was the legal advisor for Cart-Rite; see Chapter 3), got it going with three small trucks. Greenaway took off soon, and Grange diluted the ownership, with majority control in his own pocket, to Craig Symons, a friend from Leaside who was the son of a top Gulf Oil of Canada Limited executive, and Barry Dantzic, son of a Toronto policeman and a former policeman himself. David Davies later bought a piece of the company. His shares were placed in his father's name.

Grange and his friends learned about business quickly. One associate from those days remembers Grange picked up cartage contracts for his company from anywhere, sometimes undercutting competitors so much that he made no money himself. The idea was to use one contract to open more doors to new business.

As related in Chapter 2, the Toronto milk-drivers' strike and lockout in early 1970 was Grange's entry into strikebreaking. When Dominion Dairies and other milk producers called for more drivers, Grange dipped into the netherworld of crime to come up with his crews. Not everyone was as pleased as Grange with his new sideline, soon to become his principal vocation. Key personnel, who saw Cart-Rite being milked of its drivers and potential, deserted Grange. "At the time I left," recalls one of these, "Rick seemed to be replacing the guys with some intelligence with just thugs." He thought the risks were too great and the potential for open confrontation too dangerous. In the beginning, he states, violence was not part of the recipe. That soon changed. "When somebody followed you in a car, the idea was to lose 'em, not to lure 'em to the boondocks and work 'em over."

In 1972 Grange was paying his drivers $4 an hour, but in the early days he paid just $2.25 or $2.50 an hour. His recruits were happy to get it. "These guys can't work for anybody else," remarks a former Driver Pool heavy.

Although he worked them killing hours, they could make a lot of money. And money was their motivation, the only motivation.

His own motives are less clear. Clearly Grange wants money, like all professional strikebreakers, but he also covets power. His own powers of hyperbole reveal a man intensely infatuated with his own image.

He justifies his parasitic profession by elevating it with rhetoric to an art. A front-page feature story in the *Toronto Star* in 1971 revealed that, like any egotist, Grange idolizes himself. "I almost threw up when I read that quote about him in the *Star* how he does everything an artist's way," says a former Grange strikebreaker who knows him well.

Former friends believe Grange's vanity and brashness are cosmetics for insecurity. "It's not money, it's power he wants," recalls one former colleague. "Rick wants to be in a position where he can never be hurt again," says a friend. "He said he wanted as much power as the Teamsters' union," another remembers.

"He wants people to say 'Rick Grange, I know that name,' " is the way another summarizes him. "He wanted to be a millionaire by the time he was 30," says Craig Symons, a one-time partner in the cartage business. He accelerated his goal later and told one writer he expected to make his first million by the time was 28.[9]

Grange has a deep streak of conceit in his personality. In a story by legislative correspondent Harold Greer in November, 1971, Grange was quoted as saying he is "determined to give my life if necessary" to stamp out international unionism. He also considered himself "not interested in money" and described Driver Pool as "not a profit-making organization".

His friends and former strikebreakers say Grange has no distinct political philosophy and rarely talks about politics.

But he has begun attacking the New Democratic Party by name in his speeches. "I know he was certainly glad to see the Conservative Party win the last election," a one-time business aide reports.

Grange told one newspaper that "daily threats were made against him" and that a bullet had been fired at his car. (The police have no report of the alleged shooting.) In the same story he claimed, "I am basically an ordinary person. I am not physical."[10] Grange admitted he used Doberman pinschers at picket lines—instead of guns.

Grange does know how to use guns to make a point. Robert Soviak, a radio-store owner who has sold Grange thousands of dollars of tape recorders, "bugs" and other electronic equipment, explained how at Grange's wiretap trial. Soviak testified he was at Grange's branch office in the Weston Road high-rise shortly after the Driver Pool president's arrest. "Well, we were talking," Soviak related. "He got charged with wiretapping, and I said, 'I don't want to be involved in anything.' He said like, 'Don't say anything about it. Keep your mouth shut.' "[11] Soviak told the police later that Grange advised him to check his telephone "to see if it was tapped". Soviak also related, "He told me the police had one of the tape recorders I had bought for him. . . . During this time Grange was playing with a pistol in a holder which he had in his hand."[12] At the trial Soviak said although the weapon looked like a real gun, "I concluded in my own mind it was a toy gun."[13]

Former members of the Driver Pool gang say guns are traded, bought and sold within the group, trucked across the border from the United States, stashed in vehicles, kept in Driver Pool strikebreakers' apartments, and were fired regularly in mass shoot-outs for target practice in the Pool's former warehouses at 28 Tangiers Road and 257 Bridgeland Avenue and at the Oak Street base. "The inside of the warehouse looks like a sieve," is how one strikebreaker describes the impact of the gun battles with invisible invaders. The father of Brian Bertram, the young sidekick of Grange's who dropped out of school to join the strikebreaking business, was almost a victim of the free use of arms in the Driver Pool compound. According to one report, the older man drove through the gates one night and got the barrel of a gun shoved into his car. "Was there ever a lot of shit about that," one strikebreaker recalls.

Another time during a typical Saturday afternoon warehouse shoot-out, bullets sailed through the window of a nearby building. Had it been a business day the building would have been occupied, and "somebody could have been killed", according to an eyewitness.

The guns that former strikebreakers say they saw and heard discussed in Driver Pool warehouses include U.S. Army M-1s, the kind used in Vietnam, .22 calibre rifles, AR-15s, machine guns, sawed-off shotguns and assorted hand guns.

The Driver Pool arsenal would be accumulated on regular Saturday "gun hunts", as one insider calls them. Grange's crew are enamoured of weapons. Peter Paynter, for instance, used to keep a carbine in the high-rise apartment he shared with Nicholas Kerr, another Pool regular. Paynter is a reputed one-time mercenary who was expelled from the British Army. To him, Driver Pool is the army all over again. On one of his gun hunts he apparently bought a telescopic sight for a rifle and observed in the enthusiasm of a boy with a new hockey stick that it "would be good for Pool". One former strikebreaker at Driver Pool says Grange boasts he can "get anything", guns, airplanes, even bombs, from sources in the United States.

But guns are just the accoutrements of a private army, a symptom of the strikebreaker psychology, and do not explain the phenomenon. Professional strikebreakers today as always are hired to bully workers who have banded together to improve their standard of living. The most simple understanding of the psychology of the bully makes it plain why the strikebreaking profession uses them almost exclusively for the dirty work managements won't do themselves. "Bullies are not calculating and cool, effective and impressive, although some of them occasionally give the appearance," says psychologist Hans Toch. "The bully makes his own task easier by not risking even encounters. He picks on weak people because the effects of terror are most easily secured with them. . . ."[14] The tough employed to drive a truck across a picket line knows his work is hurting others, and he gets a thrill from it. "I get sort of a high out of this, you know," said a chain-wielding strikebreaker during the 1971 Texpack Limited strike in Brantford, Ontario. "I like exciting jobs."[15] He was charged with possession of an offensive weapon.

"What matters to the bully," says psychologist Toch, "is not that violence 'works', but that it impresses and damages and intimidates."[16] The use of guns, the featherbedding Driver Pool guards "riding shotgun" on scab trucks and the Pool's alacrity in calling the police when it suits the strikebreakers' purposes (as, for instance, when they want to move a truck), all indicate that paradoxically the bully, underneath the tough-talking crust, is extremely afraid. "One generally assumes that this type of alien disposition must spring from very strong motives which push the person to abandon otherwise universally held premises and feelings," says Toch, a student of violence and its practitioners. "The most probable motivating force is intense fear."[17]

So with the need to secure themselves with guns, fierce dogs and other trappings of power, they congregate for the security of a brutal brotherhood, and the camaraderie of a gang. Grange typifies the strikebreakers he employs by following the pattern of the bully. It's a role he obviously enjoys.

In the preliminary hearing for his wiretap trial, one of his former aides in Cart-Rite Cartage said he was anxious about testifying against his former associate. "Presenting evidence against Mr. Grange there's a chance of physical occurrences or things," said the man. "He has a habit of carrying on vendettas against people who intend to do him harm or try and do him harm. I've seen this occur in the past."[18] At the trial, another one-time strikebreaker with Driver Pool, Greg Ross, testified he was afraid to go to the police with information on Grange and the Driver Pool operation. "I was afraid for my own personal safety and my wife's," he told prosecutor Frank Armstrong. "What gave rise to that?" asked Armstrong. "Just knowing Mr. Grange," Ross replied.[19]

Grange's courage wanes on occasions when he's clearly outnumbered, say former strikebreakers who have worked with him. Driving across a picket line at Dominion Glass during a 1971 strike in a chase car, Grange "froze right up", according to the strikeguard who had to manoeuvre the car through a crowd of strikers. During the strike at W. J. Mowat Cartage in 1970, Grange and more than a dozen of his troops were barricaded inside the company's yard as angry strikers massed outside the gate. Seemingly overpowered, Grange put a sidekick to work finding someone who would fly in a helicopter to rescue the scabs.

The atmosphere of violence, guns, terror, fear and intrigue that surrounds the professional strikebreaking business in Ontario makes ties between the racket and organized crime a strong possibility. At least one Ontario Police Commission investigator, for example, believes that organized crime syndicates would like to muscle in on the professional strikebreaking business in Canada and elsewhere. To some degree the Mafia may already have been successful. Late in 1971, for instance, in New York City three reputed members of an organized crime syndicate were charged with extorting money from Mobil Oil Corporation, which had hired them as strikebreakers in spring that year. Company executives were told they had to make payoffs to the strikebreakers or "it'll be like the Thirties. . . ." The company paid them $72,000, the police say, of $200,000 the strikebreakers had demanded. Sular Enterprises, Incorporated, agreed to do the trucking during a drivers' strike that began May 1. Typical of the professional strikebreaking racket, the drivers were to be paid substantially more than the strikers had been bargaining for, $10 an hour. The strikebreaking agency was headed by Lazzaro Sangiovanni, who was charged with grand larceny and conspiracy with Modesto Santoro and Carmine Franzese.[20]

The goal of organized crime in the strikebreaking business is undoubtedly wider than the generous rakeoffs that scab trucks and strikeguards provide. After worming into legitimate businesses, the organized crime figures could "recommend" struck companies do business with mob-run suppliers, for instance.

The exploits of the Driver Pool heavies are not as bizarre as the wide-scale mayhem provided by the turn-of-the-century armies of Pinkerton's and latter-day industrial wrecking crews. But not surprisingly in such a group, crime has occurred in their own midst. In the summer of 1971 at the Oak Street facility called Pro-Con Consolidated Warehousing, about 100 pieces of stereo and hi-fi equipment worth $16,000 disappeared. Grange reported them stolen. The insurance companies represented by Henderson and Legge, Grange's long-time insurance agents, refused to pay.

The manufacturer, Morse Electro Products Corp. (Canada) Limited, has filed suit against Pro-Con, charging the loss was the result of "inadequate supervision", "failure to exercise necessary care and diligence" and breach of contract.

Grange, through his lawyer, has denied the warehouse is responsible for the alleged loss of the stereos.

Driver Pool employees were investigated for the alleged theft but not charged. Grange told Morse after the stereos disappeared that he didn't go to the police immediately because he thought the disappearance was an "inside job" and felt he could clear up the case himself.

Apart from the cavalier use of guns and other activities, so many of them illegal, the professional strikebreakers are not much different in their attitudes towards organized labour and working people from the rest of the population. The strikebreakers, like others who are not union members, believe generally that what they hear from Richard Grange is true. Grange's own knowledge of unions is that of almost anyone: confused, ill-informed, suspicious. The strikebreaker considers the striker his enemy. The worker is something to fear, to hold in contempt. Grange, according to a one-time close friend, "hates workers". Another remembers disgustedly that Grange talked about "the peasants".

Overt anti-unionism, even among strikebreakers, as among the public at large, is considered boorish. It is necessary to declare, as Grange did in one series of his sales letter to management: ". . . Unions have served a useful purpose in protecting the employees from unjust treatment and have helped improve working conditions. In most cases, I believe their usefulness has been out-lived and they now have become a detriment to both employees and employer."

A sales letter signed by Grange in 1972 used his gift for prevarication. "Canadian Driver Pool is neither anti-labour nor anti-union," he said. "Our basic and long-term objective is to bring management and labour together in a partnership which will assist both to achieve their goals."

Grange has no knowledge of the intricacies of industrial relations, but that doesn't stop his handing out advice to his clients. After all, he bills them for "consulting" among the regular services like guards, trucks and cameramen. A typical manual for employers prepared by Driver Pool even includes a suggested speech for company presidents to give the workers before a strike begins. The speech announces the company's intention "to operate its' [sic] business as usual, and we have made extensive plans to do so". It goes on to say how "it is not necessary for me to remind you . . . that our Company must be a good place to work. Many of you have been here for some time and have recommended your friends and relatives to us, who [sic] we have helped and employed." Grange's speech ends with an offer "to let you off for the rest of the afternoon" and adds the inducement that "you will be paid for the full eight hours today. I repeat, you will receive a full days [sic] pay for today."

By mid-1972 only one company apparently had tried out the speech. The United Steelworkers of America used the president's address as evidence to prove unfair labour practice charges against the company before the Ontario Labour Relations Board.

The misanthrope who turns strikebreaker is common. A man recruited by the Office Overload contract labour shop in

Ottawa said he had no sympathy at all for the striking garbage-men. "They don't waste any sympathy on me when I'm out of work anyway, so why should I bother about them?" the man whined. He added that strikebreaking work was a change of pace in his life style. "It's my first legal money in a long time."[21]

It helps when profit coincides with the strikebreaker's personal moral convictions. One of the first scabs recruited by Grange in the 1969 Toronto milk-drivers' strike recalls "... I was hard up for money, and he offered me a job at reasonable pay."

Not all new Driver Pool toughs are recruited from the province's jail system. Some stop by on their way in to jail. "I had a couple of weeks to go before I went to the pokey," remembers one former strikebreaker. So he went to work for Driver Pool on strike duty.

Typically, the professional strikebreaker knows little about the strike he's breaking and couldn't care less. "The morality of it did bother me a little," says a former Driver Pool strike-guard, "but when you're making two bucks an hour and some-body's on strike making six bucks an hour, you figure, well, you gotta eat too." Driver Pool never has been called in by a management paying $6 an hour. But the Grange employee is a rare one who considers the issues and weighs the righteous-ness of invading a particular strike. "It depends on the situation," one says. "If they're [the strikers] already well paid and going on strike, then my sympathy's with management."

Young Brian Bertram, who left school just out of his teens to join Grange, intended to go back to classes. But, according to a colleague at Driver Pool, "he found out he was making too much money and having too much fun".

Only one ex-Driver Pool employee acknowledges another side to the dispute besides management's, the side that hired Driver Pool. "It made me good money," says this man, "but I wasn't in favour of it." (He had been roped in by Grange to run a cartage business and was shuffled to strike work when Grange took on so much that he neglected the legitimate trucking.) "I wasn't against the unions, I didn't care. I probably rationalized it by saying it didn't hurt the men, it helped by saving the jobs." It is a favourite justification from the professional strikebreaker that keeping management's profits flowing during a strike doesn't destroy the union or force the employees to take less than management can afford. Quite the contrary, the union-busting saves the jobs or else the company would be ruined. (That was precisely the argument former Labour Minister Dalton Bales gave when the Labour Council of Metropolitan Toronto asked him in 1971 to outlaw strikebreaking.) Like a sizeable portion of the public doused with strike stories by their newspapers, radio and television, this strikebreaker says, "I still think there are too many strikes."

He agrees with Grange that "the unions are too powerful—they're hurting the people". He admits, though, "I didn't know too much about the issues." In one strike where he bothered to find out, Kenroc Tools Limited in Toronto, he found the striking employees "were grossly underpaid".

That admission will never come from Driver Pool's president, however. To Grange, the union negotiators are almost as contemptible as the workers they represent. The union bargainer "simply does not understand or appreciate management's problems", Grange said in a 1972 speaking engagement. "He does not comprehend the simple principle that his employer must keep the labour costs of his product in line with those of his competitors if he is to be able to continue in business." Why is the union leader so stupid? Because "to a large degree", Grange observed, "the union organizer or business agent comes from the ranks of the membership".[22]

The public is perhaps only a little more ambivalent about unions than is the average professional strikebreaker.

A report for the federal government's Task Force on Labour Relations in 1968 surveyed sampling results from the Canadian Institute of Public Opinion and showed that the public has no "coherent or systematic critical philosophy of unions". Among the concepts offered to back up the public's opinions against labour were too many strikes, "dictatorial leadership, excessive power, excessive agitation and demands and rackets". But, according to the task force's statistician, "none of these criticisms is held by a significant number of the public; they remain vague predispositions".[23]

In the vacuum between what the public thinks about unions and what it knows, demagogues and pseudo-experts like Grange with a stake in anti-labour agitation can insert all kinds of wild statements and falsehoods. Attacking labour, for the articulate professional strikebreaker, can anoint his work with dignity, no matter whose rights he sweeps out of the way in the process. "When I look back on my life I want to feel I have contributed something to the world, to Canada," goes a typically immodest Grange observation, "and if I can say I have shown Canadian industry how to beat the frigging international unions and helped put management and workers back into a partnership, then I think I will be able to say I have led a creative life."[24]

It would surprise Grange and others that in 50 strikes where employers were successful in smashing the unions picked by their employees since 1965, the "frigging" and "powerful" international unions were the losers in 48.[25]

Surprised but unimpressed might Grange be (and the anti-union baiters who record his manifestos on unionism and labour-management relations) that wages only infrequently mean the difference between life and death in the Canadian corporation. The Ontario Federation of Labour surveyed 138 plant shut-downs and mass lay-offs in 12 months of 1970 and 1971 and found only 5 employers who blamed high wages or labour costs for closing all or part of operations.

The O.F.L.'s plant-closure study exonerated union wage goals from blame for creating the country's chronically high unemployment. It also quoted such authorities as Eric Kierans, the former federal Liberal cabinet minister and Montreal Stock Exchange president, who backed the unions' view. Canada's branch-plant economy is full of potentially "unprofitable" plants that remain critical to the over-all profits, big profits, of the multi-national corporations who dominate the economy. ". . . A subsidiary could lose money and still make a net contribution to the parent company's income," says Kierans, "by the profit on purchases of raw materials and component parts from the parents, by patents, royalties and fees for management, advertising and research services. . . . The primary purpose of investment in overseas markets is to earn a profit for the parent by the control of markets and for the export of parts, components and raw material concentrates. It is not essential the affiliate show a profit."[26]

Overlooked in the big-wage myth perpetrated by Grange and used by his type to justify their business is that companies routinely raise wages just to keep unions out. Marsland Engineering Company Limited in Waterloo, Ontario, to cite one example, jacked up wages more than 50 per cent in one year—60 cents an hour in some cases—to try to beat off the United Electrical, Radio and Machine Workers of America.[27] The union finally was certified and negotiated a contract. But the company top-management refused to sign it. The union took the company before the Ontario Labour Relations Board on unfair labour-practice charges twice and got consent to prosecute Marsland in provincial court both times.

(For breaking the U.E., Marsland was fined $250, its

president $50. The union took the company to court again, but the case was thrown out on a technicality although the witnesses and testimony were identical to those at the first trial. A third application for consent to prosecute was made to the O.L.R.B. but withdrawn when the determination of the workers to strike ran out, says Ross Russell, U.E.'s director of organization. The work force, largely women, had turned over almost completely. The union was broken. "The workers are going to have to learn to fight," Russell says bitterly. "The courts aren't going to do it for them.")

At Welland, Ontario, Atlas Steel Company boosted wages to levels paid by the unionized Steel Company of Canada Limited, an increase of $1.27 an hour in three years, to beat back successfully an organizing drive by the United Steelworkers of America in 1970.[28]

Grange changed his line slightly in 1972 after his conviction on wiretap-conspiracy charges with a Toronto police constable and after sudden interest by the press. No doubt showing the influence of his public-relations counsellor, James Tannian, Grange was declaring, "I wouldn't say we are strikebreakers. We are more along the line of strike preventers."[29]

Grange, of course, cannot prove that his work has prevented a single strike. But certainly professional strikebreaking like his has extended many. Two-thirds of the strikes where Driver Pool was involved lasted longer than the 1970 national average for all strikes and lockouts in the country (27 days). According to figures kept by the provincial and federal Labour Departments, only 4 per cent of all strikes last more than 100 working days. But 21 per cent of the Driver Pool strikes lasted more than 100 days—five times as many as walkouts free of strikebreaking.

One could almost hear the notorious American scab herder Pearl L. Bergoff looking over Grange's shoulder. "I can see so much strife ahead I don't know which way to turn. There'll be more strikes in 1935 than ever in history, and it don't make me mad."[30]

Notes

1. Wolf, Herman, "Strike-Breaker Number One," *The Nation*, November 13, 1935, p. 568.
2. *Violations of Free Speech and Rights of Labour*, Report of the U.S. Senate Committee on Education and Labour (La Follette committee), Report No. 46, Part 3, 76th Congress, 1939, p. 65.

3. *Ibid.,* p. 66.
4. *Ibid.,* p. 86.
5. *Toronto Daily Star,* November 20, 1971, p. 13.
6. Greer, Harold, "Strike-buster a dedicated anti-unionist," *The London Free Press,* November 8, 1971.
7. *Toronto Daily Star,* February 11, 1969.
8. *Toronto Daily Star,* December 6, 1969, and December 4, 1969.
9. *Toronto Daily Star,* November 20, 1971.
10. *North York* (Ontario) *Mirror/Enterprise,* November 24, 1971, p. 1.
11. Her Majesty the Queen vs. Barry Chapman and Richard Grange (Preliminary Hearing Transcript) Provincial Court (Criminal Division), County of York, pp. 322-323.
12. *Ibid.,* p. 330.
13. *Ibid.,* p. 334.
14. Toch, Hans, *Violent Men, An Inquiry into the Psychology of Violence,* Aldine Publishing Company, Chicago, 1969, p. 161.
15. *Toronto Daily Star,* September 4, 1971, p. 25.
16. Toch, *op. cit.,* p. 161.
17. *Ibid.,* p. 160.
18. Preliminary transcript, *op. cit.,* pp. 137-138.
19. Trial transcript, *op. cit.,* p. 302.
20. *The New York Times,* December 10, 1971, pp. 1, 86.
21. *The Ottawa Citizen,* August 12, 1971, p. 37.
22. *The* (Brockville, Ontario) *Recorder and Times,* May 6, 1972, p. 3.
23. March, R. R., *Public Opinion and Industrial Relations,* Privy Council Office, Ottawa, 1968, p. 13.
24. *Toronto Daily Star,* November 20, 1971, p. 13.
25. Survey by the Ontario Federation of Labour, 1972.
26. In 93 plants, the employees were represented by unions. About one-half were total shutdowns of operations, according to John W. Eleen, the research director of the O.F.L. The survey is reported in *Shutdown: The Impact of Plant Shutdown, Extensive Employment Terminations and Layoffs on the Workers and the Community,* by Eleen and Ashley G. Bernardine.
27. *U.E. News,* November 17, 1969.
28. *St. Catharines* (Ontario) *Standard,* March 9, 1970.
29. *Toronto Daily Star,* May 15, 1972, p. 8.
30. *Fortune, op. cit.,* p. 92.

5

With a Lot of Help from my Friends

"You see, in this line of work they never asked for no references."

Sam "Chowderhead" Cohen, a famous strikebreaker, commenting on his long criminal record.[1]

The Toronto-based strikebreaking organization of Richard Grange was formed under the nose—or under the wing—of the Ontario Department of Labour. The Labour Department at the highest levels sanctioned Grange's entry into the strike-breaking field. From official Labour Department records, he was able to contact presidents of companies in bargaining and offer to break their strikes or infiltrate their unions.

That a supposedly neutral government department should turn aggressor against labour by opening the path to Grange and other professional strikebreakers may be considered illegal or immoral, but it is not surprising. Professional strikebreaking can exist only under the auspices of business and government. In the case of Grange's Canadian Driver Pool, those in government aiding him include the Metropolitan Toronto Police, the Ontario Provincial Police, the court system, the Department of Transportation, the Department of Labour, the Department of Financial and Commercial Affairs and the Office of the Attorney-General.

The help of a few individuals in critical positions who are willing to be corrupted, intimidated, compromised and used by an industrial soldier of fortune has given professional strikebreaking in Ontario a terrifying and dangerous stature.

It is not fair to say that entire police forces or government agencies have becomed entangled in the squalid business of professional strikebreaking and anti-union espionage. Guilt by association, as U.S. Supreme Court Justice William O. Douglas has said, "is a dangerous doctrine. It condemns one man for the unlawful conduct of another. It draws ugly insinuations from an association that may be wholly innocent."[2]

However, it is not the many who labour honestly in police uniforms or at government desks whose reputations are tainted by the few who have actively assisted or encouraged strikebreaking to the extent that it has reached a significant threat to public law and order. Rather, it is the few politicians, civil servants and others with responsibilities to the public at large who have defiled the reputations of many good people by letting themselves become part of a growing public menace.

The first official blessing the Progressive Conservative Government of Ontario gave Richard Grange was in September, 1970. Grange had applied a month earlier to incorporate Canadian Driver Pool Limited. In the companies branch of the Department of Financial and Commercial Affairs in Toronto, an official, C. A. Mulla, sent a copy of Grange's application to the Labour Department. Department Solicitor Frank G. Harrington of the Labour Department wrote back on September 10, 1970: "We have reviewed the objects of the proposed company and have found no conflict with the statutes administered by our Department." Harrington's reply was not unique since the government then and now considers professional strikebreaking and anti-union espionage perfectly legal.

What was unusual about the Labour Department official's reply is that from the time the letter from the companies branch arrived in the legal department on the morning of September 4, 1970, it took less than five business days for the Labour Department to decide that Canadian Driver Pool Limited was no threat to collective bargaining, public welfare or stable industrial relations in Ontario.

The purposes of the company were stated this way on the application for incorporation:

(a) to acquire the right to the services of and to employ other persons in any and all fields of endeavor and to contract and deal with others with respect to the services of any such persons;

(b) to render managerial, supervisory or other services to and to advise with respect to the business or operations of and to take part in the formation, management, supervision, control or liquidation of the business or operations of any other company, corporation, firm, business or undertaking of any nature or kind and wheresoever carried on.

Notwithstanding that the avowed purposes of the company as set out in its application were so amorphous as to be virtually meaningless, and ignoring the publicity the company's strike-breaking efforts have generated since early 1971, neither the Labour Department, which sanctioned Driver Pool, nor the Financial and Commercial Affairs Department, which ratified its formation, has considered reviewing the application. Frank G. Harrington, the solicitor, has since left the Labour Department under mysterious circumstances. He lives as a virtual recluse in tiny Wawa, a town in northern Ontario northwest of Sault Ste. Marie. Harrington is a Queen's Counsel, a distinction conferred annually by the Attorney-General on a select group of lawyers.

The official story of why the companies branch referred the Driver Pool application to the Labour Department is that such a procedure was "routine". "For your information, where the objects in an application for incorporation appear to relate to an activity which may be regulated by legislation by a department of the Government the Companies Branch advises the Department which in turn examines the objects to see if they are in breach of such legislation," Paul Hess, Harrington's successor at the department, stated in 1972. Hess was writing to Ralph Forsey, president of the local union at Redpath Sugars Limited, where Driver Pool had worked the year before.

Why the application from a company called "Driver Pool" that stated its business was to "render managerial, supervisory or other services" would not be referred to the Department of Transportation, which regulates drivers, remains a mystery to this day. Why an application to incorporate a company that made no reference to employees, employers, unions or any other groups directly affected by legislation administered by the Labour Department should be referred to the solicitor's office in that department also remains a mystery.

Hess's subtle-toned letter to Forsey of the Redpath union on April 7, 1972, was in distinct contrast with his tone with a private investigator hired by the International Chemical Workers' Union to dig into the strikebreaking at Redpath. Max Chikofsky, the investigator, says that when he tried to talk with Harrington about the Driver Pool application Hess called and "blew his stack". Hess literally shouted at Chikofsky over the telephone, the investigator says, and demanded to know what he aimed to find out and why he was trying to find Hess's predecessor. Hess claimed he had talked with Harrington, Chikofsky states. In May, 1972, Chikofsky submitted a list of detailed questions on the Driver Pool application to the companies branch of the Department of Financial and Commercial Affairs. Officials there refused to answer. The "routine" form referring Driver Pool's application to the Labour Department has disappeared from the company's file.

One question Chikofsky tried futilely to get answered was how extensively Driver Pool and its founder were investigated by the Labour Department, the Financial and Commercial Affairs Department, anybody, in fact, before the company was allowed to incorporate.

It is obvious that had Harrington dispatched the Labour Department's special investigator, R. G. Chappel, or had anyone probed even slightly into the murky affairs of Driver Pool, it would have been disclosed that Grange was already sending out his promotion letters while the application to incorporate was still on Harrington's desk. It would have become obvious that Grange was offering a security-guard service that he didn't have a licence to provide. It may have occurred to someone, had anyone wanted to find out, that Grange was assembling a private army of what the labour movement commonly calls "goons". The Labour Department could have asked what sort of "managerial, supervisory or other services" Grange intended to sell. But Grange's favoured treatment by the Labour Department didn't end with the endorsement he got from the legal branch.

The Labour Department's research branch publishes an annual listing of the dates when all union contracts expire in Ontario under the provincial jurisdiction, and the union and company involved. Primarily it's for the use of legitimate researchers in labour relations, for the department's own conciliation and mediation branch and a few newspaper reporters who regularly cover the labour beat.

The book, a thick document with a blue cover and plastic binding, is considered an internal, almost confidential, document. The Metropolitan Toronto Police could not get it. The consulting firm of Hedlin-Menzies Associates Limited, which has done hundreds of thousands of dollars in work for the provincial government and has dealt regularly and intimately with high Labour Department officials, could not get it. Richard Grange got it. For him it became a crucial part of his business.

How he got the first list is unclear. How he got the second and third is easier to explain. One former strikebreaker who sent out Grange's letters says, "I called the Labour Department and said, 'It's Canadian Driver Pool calling; where's your book of contracts?' " One arrived shortly in the mail, he says. The book lists only the names of companies. Grange wanted to write directly to the presidents. A directory of city businesses in Metropolitan Toronto was used from the public library. For out-of-town presidents' names, says a former Driver Pool employee, "I called the company and said, 'This is the Department of Labour calling. Will you tell me the name of your president?' "

Companies just organized by unions would not appear in the Labour Department's compendium of contracts. Companies that are dealing with a union for the first time are considered particularly good potential clients by professional strikebreakers. Grange gets the names of these companies from a list of new unions published regularly by the Ontario Labour Relations Board. The board certifies all new unions in the province that can prove they represent the majority of workers in a plant or office and reports new certifications once or twice a month.

The Labour Department is used in other, less obvious, ways. A salesman for Horn's Provisioners Limited, the home-freezer business owned by James Patry, a partner in Driver Pool, called on at least one member of the Ontario Labour Relations Board in 1972 to try to get the names of unions likely to be on strike. The object, said the man from Horn's, was to sell the union members the plan to stock a freezer in their homes, with no payments until the strike was over. He also reportedly saw at least one member of the conciliation and mediation branch to get the same information. Information on upcoming strikes naturally would be useful to Patry's business partner, Richard A. Grange. While Grange prolonged their strike, the union members could be eating Patry's food.

(Ironically, perhaps, American scab king Pearl L. Bergoff also had a sidekick in the food business. In big strikes when hundreds of Bergoff goons had to be quartered and fed, Bergoff turned almost always to the Washington Beef Company of New York City, which provided cooks and food for a flat sum. Bergoff once claimed the food company made a million dollars by following Bergoff strikebreakers for 25 years.)[3]

One manufacturer reported to a negotiator for the United Steelworkers of America in 1972 that he would consider using Grange if the union struck. He told the union man that during a sales talk with company executives Grange claimed to have "tremendous influence" with the Department of Labour. The executives were impressed. Grange did not elaborate.

Not only the Labour Department but also the Department of Transportation has gone easy on Driver Pool and other strike-breakers by letting them circumvent the Public Commercial Vehicles Act. The P.C.V. Act requires that companies hauling someone else's goods must be licenced. But some companies that can't get licences in the crowded cartage business set up dummy corporations, one to lease trucks to clients, which call the trucks their own, and another front to supply drivers. Proving that the two companies are one and the same occasionally can be difficult. In 1970 Grange was listed as treasurer of Driver Pool and Intercontinental Container Leasing Limited. I.C.L. was fined $50 in December, 1971, for operating without a commercial vehicle licence. Fifty-dollar fines obviously are not eradicating the practice, but the Transport Department has done nothing to toughen the law. Judges, however, are inclined sometimes to see things more simply. When a similar case of a company renting a truck and a driver to get through the loophole in the law was brought before a judge in Windsor, Ontario, in 1971, the judge didn't hesitate to call the deal "a sham agreement". The judge added, "It is obvious this is a thinly disguised haulage contract."[4]

The Transportation Department's listless enforcement of its own laws to curtail unlicenced trucking is also a stab in the back of the labour movement. Most of the truck-leasing companies employ temporary drivers. They are often recruited from contract-labour shops, the same "labour slave-markets" that regularly refer scabs to struck plants. Because the drivers technically are not employees, but sub-contractors, they cannot be unionized. The unlicenced haulage companies could cause upheaval in the entire truck industry, warned Ray Taggart, the Hamilton, Ontario, leader of the International Brotherhood of Teamsters who died in August, 1972. The Teamsters, said Taggart, bargain for merely half the amount of the trucking industry that the union did 10 years ago. "We've been to Shoniker [E. J. Shoniker, chairman of the Ontario Highway Transport Board] time after time," says Charles Thibault, president of the big Toronto-based Teamster Local 938. "He just shrugs and says there's nothing he can do about it."

The Transportation Department aparently doesn't know that Grange's cars used by Canadian Driver Pool to deliver scabs were registered fraudulently as owned by Metro Car Lease Limited in 1972. According to the companies branch of the

Department of Financial and Commercial Affairs, no such company exists. Metro Car Lease Limited's address on the registration for two station wagons was listed as 2240 Weston Road, the same address as Canadian Driver Pool's branch office, radio centre and photographic operation. In 1971 one of the vehicles had been registered to Driver Pool, the other to Intercontinental Container Leasing. Grange claims to own Metro Car Lease, according to the Ontario Provincial Police and a former employee of Driver Pool. There was also no record that Metro Car Lease was a subsidiary of any other Grange operation at the time cars were being registered to the purported leasing company. Its purpose was to lease cars to Grange's clients. The strikeguards and other toughs hired to police the strike would occupy and drive the leased cars.

The hands-off policies of the Labour and Transportation Departments towards Canadian Driver Pool and its ancillary companies were also followed obediently by the Department of Financial and Commercial Affairs. From the beginning they let pass Driver Pool's application for incorporation while, according to former employees, it was already functioning. They have also excused the use of the legally-restricted term "limited" by two purported subsidiaries of the Grange web of companies, Metro Car Lease and Pro-Con Consolidated Warehousing. Financial and Commercial Affairs officials have also neglected, in Grange's case, to enforce the laws on disclosure and the filing of annual returns about the structure of companies registered in Ontario. Grange himself was originally a director and secretary-treasurer of Driver Pool. But when he was arrested in October, 1971, for conspiracy to wiretap a union strike office, he called himself president. No record of the change in corporate officers could be found at the Department of Financial and Commercial Affairs, though every change in the executive makeup of a company must be reported by law to the department just after it occurs. The latest corporate return, similarly, for Cart-Rite Cartage, which shows Grange as president, also shows two partners, Robert Davies as secretary and W. Craig Symons as vice-president. Both have sold their interest in the company, but this fact was not reported to the Department of Financial and Commercial Affairs as late as almost a year after the ownership changed. Corporate disclosures about Cart-Rite required by law to be filed annually were not in the public records of the department when searched in May, 1972.

In the Department of Justice, too, government employees and

other officials responsible to the Attorney-General of the province have helped Richard Grange to build a formidable clientele.

It became apparent soon after Grange's operations (which had been relatively unknown for more than a year) were reported in June, 1971, that Driver Pool was offering a security-guard service. Security guards and private investigators in Ontario and most other provinces have to hold licences. Neither Grange nor any of his companies had a security licence. The Justice Department, nevertheless, steadfastly refused to prosecute Grange despite an ever-mounting agglomeration of evidence that he was offering and providing guards and investigators. In his original promotion letters that went out as early as 1970, Grange was promising "a separate security division", which he modestly called "the most experienced organization in this field on the North American Continent". He claimed his men and his dogs "are trained for crowd control and plant security". No charges were laid. The Private Investigators and Security Guards Act provides that every person who breaks the law is liable to a $2,000 fine and a year's prison sentence. A corporation found guilty of breaking the law on guards could be fined $25,000. Unlike most laws, no prosecutions under the investigators' and guards' legislation can be started without the consent of the Justice Department. No charges were laid by May, 1972, although repeated complaints had been made to the Ontario Provincial Police, who enforce the act, and directly to the office of the man who was Attorney-General and Minister of Justice through much of Driver Pool's life, Allan F. Lawrence.

The Justice Department has the right under law—with protection for applicants to appeal—to deny a licence or rescind one if the agency, investigator or guard is deemed unsuitable. If Grange's own background were not enough to disqualify him, it is unlikely that most of his heavies could get licences or that an agency employing them could get the mandatory protection bond. Even for a party in power like the Conservatives, who tolerate and encourage strikebreaking, it probably would be too embarrassing to grant an agency licence to a company that employs as many ex-convicts as Grange does.

Grange claimed, whenever questioned about his lack of a security-agency licence, that his men only guarded trucks owned or operated by Driver Pool and its men. (An employer's own guards do not have to be licenced.) The Justice Department

79

laid off, although on many occasions Grange's toughs were not guarding his trucks and their cargoes at all but other companies' trucks that had been leased by Grange or his clients to carry out scab-made products.

Nevertheless, he did show he wanted a licence to shut off possible prosecution by a less friendly and sympathetic Justice Minister, when he applied for a licence in June, 1971.

The name Grange came up with to apply for a security licence was Canadian Specialized Services. Even before the application for Specialized Services Grange met personally with high O.P.P. officials to discuss a licence for Driver Pool, former associates say. He said of the licence in June, "I expect it to come through any day." Other applicants for the agency licence were James Patry, Driver Pool vice-president and head of Horn's Provisioners, and Nicholas D. Kerr, son of an English industrialist and a Grange cohort almost from the beginning of Driver Pool. "Any day" could have been the response expected from a government that had taken so little interest in Grange's business up until then. Time dragged on. The O.P.P. found out about Grange's criminal past while deciding what to do about the licence. Grange, conveniently for the government, got arrested on the wiretap charge for his work on behalf of Redpath Sugars in Toronto.

Grange wrote the O.P.P. on October 19, a few days after his arrest, "in light of recent events" it would be "unlikely" that he'd get his licence, and he withdrew his application. The day before, another application for a front company already had been submitted.

On the application for the front were the names of Nick Kerr, who was listed as a principal on the earlier application for "Canadian Specialized Services," and the name of James Kevin McEwan.

McEwan, a former Metropolitan Toronto traffic policeman, had moonlighted for Grange before quitting the force, according to former Driver Pool employees. While on the force he supplied Grange with run-downs on people Grange asked him to check out. In anything the two were involved in, says a friend who knows both, "Rick would be the leader, and Kevin the follower." McEwan quit the police October 11, 1971, four days before his new boss was charged in the wiretapping case with another policeman, Metro constable Barry Chapman.

McEwan tried in vain to get back on the Metro police force after Grange was arrested. He tried to enlist the help of the Metropolitan Toronto Police Association. But the Force told

McEwan he'd have to go on a waiting list, and it could take a year before his application would be considered. Police sources and spokesmen give conflicting stories about whether the one-year waiting period is an inflexible requirement or was a smoke screen to conceal the department's real reasons for not taking back McEwan. Anyway, McEwan decided to make a go of the security business, using recruits lined up for "his" company by Grange and Driver Pool. "There's nothing wrong with providing night security for a company," McEwan said later about his company's role in breaking strikes. He proceeded with the application for a security licence.

It occurred to McEwan, his lawyer, Ray G. Goodwin (who is also Grange's lawyer), and to Grange that Nick Kerr's name on the security-agency application might be a liability. Kerr had a long association with Grange and was vice-president of Driver Pool. With the president of Driver Pool due in court (this is 1972) on conspiracy charges, the application for a licence from a company at the same Weston Road office that Driver Pool was using would raise suspicions. McEwan withdrew it on February 7. Then he submitted his own application for a "new" company, Canadian Specialized Security Limited. To cover his ties with Driver Pool—and to protect the government from charges it had licenced a strikebreaker— McEwan swore out an affidavit that he was sole owner of Specialized Security. The application was expedited. Within days, orders had come "from the top", according to O.P.P. sources, to grant the licence. Grange had a front. McEwan was in business. He even bothered to rent a separate apartment, at 265 Dixon Road, No. 708, about a mile from the Driver Pool office in the high-rise.

It was true that McEwan was the sole owner of Canadian Specialized Security Limited. It was true at the time he made the affidavit and at the time the security licence was granted. But days later he agreed to sign over 75 per cent ownership in the company to Brian Legge, Grange's friend and an investor in some of Grange's enterprises. Legge did not have his own security licence, as every principal and every employee of a guard or investigation agency must possess. The affidavit McEwan had signed purporting to eschew any connection with Grange and his professional strikebreaking outfits gave the camouflage that the Justice Department wanted to defend the decision to grant McEwan's licence. That is precisely what transpired. On April 6, 1972, New Democratic Party leader Stephen Lewis raised the question. Dalton Bales, who had taken over from Lawrence as Attorney-General, declared, "There was a sworn affidavit by the applicant [McEwan] that he was the sole owner."[5] Even before Bales answered Lewis's question, the authority to sign cheques for the guard company that Bales said Grange was not connected with had been given to Ron Wilson, the bookkeeper for all the companies in the Grange complex. Clients who supposedly hired Specialized Security actually paid Driver Pool.

Though it apparently wasn't a sensitive matter for the government (they didn't seem to care really whether Grange had a licence or not), it evidently was for Grange. Snooping reporters were told in June, 1971, "We haven't been involved in any security operations during the past year. . . . All our security has been conducted through a separate outside security firm."[6]

But whatever Grange or the government said about the matter, as far as Grange's own employees were concerned Driver Pool was supplying security to struck companies. The preliminary transcript and the court record of Grange's wiretap-conspiracy trial are laced with references by former employees to security work. The implication is plain that they felt they were doing more than guarding Grange's trucks or each other.

Peter Paynter, the bearded gun-lover, was described by a former employee, for example, as "head of security" for Driver Pool.[7] David B. Davies, one of Grange's former partners in Cart-Rite Cartage Limited, described his own work this way: ". . . Basically I did both driving, organized some of the security and tried to keep—keep the operation flowing smoothly."

Grange himself posed as a private investigator, the trial was told. The manager of a radio-equipment store where Grange purchased tape recorders recalled, "I was talking to him why he wanted two of them instead of one. What would he be doing with two? . . . He told me that he was a private investigator and he required these tape recorders for investigation."[8]

Companies, too, considered Grange in the security business—for them. Edward J. Brady, manager of labour relations for Kimberly-Clark of Canada, which used Driver Pool in 1971 during a strike, said that even before the strike the paper company had "talked to him about security matters at some of our other mills. . . ."[9] Brady explained that when the St. Catharines operation of the company was struck, ". . . we wanted someone around besides our own watchman on each shift."[10] Grange's guards punched a clock "as watchmen usually do", and how many guards were needed "was entirely up to him. . . ."[11] Driver Pool, said Brady, supplanted Anning Investigations Limited at the plant.

Just one day before the Ontario Federation of Labour was to present its annual legislative proposals to the provincial cabinet in June, 1972, the O.P.P. announced that at last it had laid charges against Driver Pool and its president for allegedly breaking the security-guard law. The original complaints relied on information about Driver Pool activities that was at least six months old.

At no time, it seems obvious, did anyone in the government *seriously* investigate what sort of business Canadian Driver Pool was or what sort of individuals composed it. Measured against what could easily have been found out from such an investigation, the statements of the government ministers involved are almost incredible. To be charitable, the ministers look foolish. Or, they could be accused of serious negligence.

Ministers of the government have consistently tried to cover up the strikebreaking issue when questioned by opposition party members in the Legislature about Canadian Driver Pool. The ministers have misled the Legislature about the timing, progress, and results of investigations. They have dissembled, whitewashed and deliberately attempted to minimize the potential danger of professional strikebreaking agencies like Driver Pool.

In June, 1971, then-Labour Minister Gordon Carton accepted at face value the claim that Driver Pool had not operated before it was incorporated. "They have only been in operation for about six months," he told the Legislature.[12]

Grange's claim that he had been involved in strikes for two years was "somewhat fantasy".[13] Carton also said that he was "not happy with the type of advertising" Grange was doing in his letters to managements. Carton said he found them "personally repugnant".[14]

But under pressure in the Legislature, Carton said he would ask the O.P.P. to investigate Driver Pool. He added glibly, "Perhaps he [Grange] is making some claims that he cannot substantiate."[15] Carton's deputy minister of labour, Thomas M. Eberlee, backed him up later in 1971 when Grange again made the headlines in the investigation of the Redpath Sugars wiretapping. "He is a baloney artist from way back," said Eberlee. "His interest now is to get in the newspaper for free publicity." Eberlee, according to the *Toronto Star*, believed Driver Pool was "really a minor operation".[16]

Sometimes ministers who got involved with Driver Pool were simultaneously contradicting themselves. Carton, as Labour Minister, was saying in December, 1971, that his investigation had uncovered nothing illegal about Driver Pool.[17] But five days later Attorney-General Lawrence wrote to the Ontario Federation of Labour that his department was "proceeding with the investigation . . . related to alleged contraventions of The Private Investigators and Security Guards Act". Because of the charge pending against Grange in the wiretap case, he said, there were "minor delays in order that our investigation may not prejudice the fair trial of the individuals".[18] Carton, however, was more eager to wash his hands of the matter, and he told the Legislature a week before, "I did a check through the Attorney-General's Department into whether or not they were offering security services. I did as complete a check as I could and in no way were they contravening the law."[19] In May, 1972, the investigation that Carton assured the Legislature had turned up nothing was continuing, according to Carton's successor in the Labour portfolio, Fernand Guindon. Guindon told the Legislature, "There is an investigation going on by the Ministry of the Attorney-General and we are supplying them with all the information we can possibly give them."[20]

Lawrence not only contradicted Carton about the investigation of Driver Pool, he even contradicted himself. In October, 1971, one week before the provincial election, and just days after the tape recorders were found by Redpath Sugars employees, Lawrence was asked by the president of the Labour Council of Metropolitan Toronto to conduct an investigation into Driver Pool's activities. This was after unionists had reported that they had discovered a tape recorder at their strike headquarters where another company, Kenroc Tools, had engaged Driver Pool. Lawrence refused to investigate and telegraphed the Labour Council President, Donald Montgomery, that Driver Pool ". . . is not subject to registration of security guard or investigator business and [is] not under jurisdiction of this department".[21] Lawrence then went back to campaigning for the October 21 election. But two months later Lawrence changed his mind, decided Driver Pool was under his jurisdiction and ordered an investigation.

(Lawrence is subject to these abrupt turnabouts. In September, 1971, speaking to a student audience during the campaign at the University of Toronto, the Justice Minister announced that "under the Ontario Labour Relations Act there is a section which can penalize companies for using strikebreakers". The next day aides called various news media to retract the comment.)[22]

There was concern over the political ramifications of the wiretap incident at the highest levels of the Tory party, according to informed sources. Chief inspector Walter L. Lidstone of the O.P.P. was assigned as Premier Davis's personal investigator on the case. But even eight months after Lidstone's special assignment was made, the Premier had not acted on Lidstone's reports.

Lawrence tried to cover himself—and the Progressive Conservative Government—at all times during the election campaign and the wiretap investigation. Metro police sources say the police wanted to proceed methodically, hoping to piece together more facts on the Redpath wiretap, the recorder found a few days earlier at Kenroc and other suspected wiretaps.

But Lawrence wanted the investigation closed right away. A quick wrap-up and charges against someone would push the wiretap business out of the headlines in the final days of the campaign. In the words of the minister's executive assistant, Lawrence wanted the probe to be "full-scale, fast and right now".[23] Detectives John Laybourne and William Kerr were able to oblige under pressure, and Grange and Barry Chapman, the policeman, were charged October 16, eight days after Chapman had been trapped in an alley behind the strike headquarters by Redpath workers who had set up a stake-out. Lawrence meanwhile was calling strikebreaking a "highly reprehensible labour practice" and declaring inaccurately that there were laws on the books to stop it.[24]

Just one day before the arrests Lawrence told the Steelworkers' union in a telegram that he couldn't do anything about the Kenroc wiretap unless the police were involved in setting the tap. "I am powerless to act on wiretapping," Lawrence stated.[25]

(Kerr and Laybourne, the Toronto detectives, found out a month after the arrest of Chapman and Grange that a wiretap had been placed at the union headquarters during the Kimberly-Clark strike, where Driver Pool's Peter Paynter was in charge of operations.)

What Carton, Guindon, Lawrence and their fellow ministers were saying and doing is typical of government intervention in Ontario's industrial relations. The Progressive Conservative Government has maintained endlessly that it is only a neutral party between the two sides of management and labour. Carton, Guindon and a line of predecessors in the labour portfolio have continually mouthed their "disgust" (Carton's word) or other contempt for strikebreaking but have never done anything to curtail it. They consistently have made the utterly sophomoric comparison between the right of a striker to seek another job and the "right" of the company to keep operating. Every government probe into strikebreaking in the United States (there have been three) has recommended professional strikebreaking be outlawed. So did the Ontario government's labour advisor, Justice Ivan C. Rand.

Carton pretended to understand the problem and blamed violence at picket lines on the strikebreakers. "The employees on strike are already upset and wrought up at management. If they find a company such as Canadian Driver Pool on the scene, the situation becomes volatile. You have the possibility of violence," he told a reporter in January, 1972. "These people are professionals, not people seeking jobs."[26] He then is reported to have said in disbelief, "How on earth can management put itself in that position?"

Dalton Bales, when he was Labour Minister, spelled out the Tories' philosophy on strikebreaking perhaps better than any other minister. Bales typified the aloofness that all Tories bring to the labour portfolio. The archetypal Labour Minister utters nothing but carefully measured amounts of wisdom to keep the scales "in balance"—which means tipped heavily towards the management side. Thus, in June, 1970, he commented in the Legislature that he opposed the employment of strikebreakers because their use "has not been helpful to future negotiations".[27] Three months later, however, he wrote to the Labour Council of Metropolitan Toronto: "Have you considered that it could be to the advantage of the strikers in some cases to keep the plant operating?"[28]

Union officials often concede (though rarely for attribution) that goods already in a struck plant are going to undermine the impact of a strike if management ships them. Says one union staff man: "Management has paid the employees to make the stuff, so they say they have a right to ship it. It's a tough position to argue against."

What the Tory government has refused to acknowledge is the difference between the casual scab who is so desperate that he or she will work anywhere for anything and the industrial mercenary whose livelihood depends on the continuation of the strike and the presence of turmoil, not the resolution of the bargaining process.

Even Grange's own strikebreakers discern that they are out of business if tension ebbs at the picket line and the union

and company engage in a nice, quiet strike. The Tories have yet
to admit they understand that. "A contract?" says one ex-
Driver Pool strikebreaker. "That's the last thing Rick wants
to see."

In New York State in 1959, a "special committee of investigation" was set up by the state's industrial commissioner,
M. P. Catherwood, to probe professional strikebreaking. The
three-member blue-ribbon commission had this to say refuting
the wizened argument that companies have a "right" to operate
by any means during a strike:

> When we speak of the employer's right to continue his
> business during a strike, are we not thinking of his right to
> continue to operate in the ordinary course, to hire from the
> sources usually available to him, employees who have an
> interest in their jobs as jobs, to pay these employees wages
> which approximate those he has offered to the employees
> who have struck?
>
> In our judgement this concept does not encompass the
> hire of strikebreakers through an agency which has no
> independent basis for existence.[29]

A ready pool of professional strikebreakers, the commis-
sioners concluded, tends to "withdraw employer incentive to
bargain . . . bringing about the very strike the replacements
were to insure against".[30]

A friendly government helps the professional strikebreaker.
So do friendly police. The Ontario Provincial Police were so
disinterested in the threat of professional strikebreaking in 1972
that when the man who fronted for Richard Grange's security
company, J. Kevin McEwan, told a high O.P.P. official that
he was going to fold the company, the O.P.P. inspector tried
to discourage him. Although security-company licences cannot
by law be transferred (a new application must be made by every
individual if a guard company is sold or started), an O.P.P.
official generously said he would hold onto McEwan's licence for
Canadian Specialized Security Limited to see if anyone else in
Grange's camp would come forward to pick it up. Grange began
right away to have a trusted strikebreaker, John Carrigan,
apply for the licence, says a former connection of Driver
Pool's.

The O.P.P. and the government have been just as enthusiastic
about licencing other security-guard agencies that perform strike
duties for union-hating employers. There are laws in several
states of the U.S. prohibiting the use of private security guards

in strikes. There are no restrictions in Canada. There are nearly 200 licenced security-guard agencies in Ontario and 16,000 licenced guards.[31] It is probably safe to assume that almost any agency will provide guards for an employer engaged in a labour dispute. Only the bigger ones, however, have the manpower at the ready when a boss calls for reinforcements to get scabs in or his products out. The larger guard agencies work closely with a truck-leasing company. Anning's favourite scab cargo machine for a time was Robertson Truck Rentals. Together they broke the union at Hanes Hosiery near Toronto in 1969. Another client of both was National Starch for a strike by the Oil, Chemical and Atomic Workers' International Union in 1969.

All the biggest Canadian security firms are American-owned. Pinkerton's of Canada Limited and the William J. Burns International Detective Agency both claim to be the biggest. In third place is Wackenhut Corporation. The big three operate under their own names in this country. Burns also owns S.I.S. (Security Investigation Systems) Protection Company.

Significantly, both Burns and Pinkerton decline strike work and anti-union espionage in the United States but take all they can in Canada.[32] (New York and other states carefully restrict the use of private security guards to guarding, not driving scabs or trucks.) Pinkerton's occasionally will handle guard duties at a struck plant in the U.S., but only with the consent of both the company and the striking union.[33]

Pinkerton's of Canada gets spill-over business from big American-owned corporations in Canada, like Du Pont, which retained Pinkerton strikeguards for a strike in 1972 at its Kingston operation. Pinkerton men had been standing by in every one of the last four rounds of bargaining, according to the International Chemical Workers' Union.

Stephen Lewis, the leader of the N.D.P., stated it aptly when he said that the government "is in the impossible position of having to license firms deliberately engaged in strikebreaking. . . ."[34] Anning Investigations Limited, as it was known until 1971 when owner Raymond Anning sold out to Wackenhut of the United States, probably has handled much more strike work than Grange's Driver Pool. In 1969 Anning boasted that his operatives had worked in 35 strikes in Ontario in three years. He also claimed his strikebreaking had helped his business gross $1 million in 1969 and that income was doubling every year. "Our policy is management-oriented," Anning observed.[35] Anning's men and most "rent-a-cops", as many unionists disdainfully call them, wear uniforms as required by the Security Guards Act. They are easier to spot than the plainclothes employees of Driver Pool. The uniforms of S.I.S. men are so good looking, they are regularly mistaken by the public for real policemen, says Syd Brown, president of the Metropolitan Toronto Police Association. Brown doesn't like it. Some Anning-Wackenhunt clients have included *The Windsor Star* (for a sit-in strike by production workers in 1970), Continental Can and Johnson, Matthey & Mallory (with Driver Pool), Dominion Glass (with Grange's men), AP Parts with scab truckers from Extra Driver Services), Proctor-Silex in Picton, Ontario (where the union was broken) and Bach-Simpson Limited in London, Ontario (where the company smashed a 90-member local of the International Brotherhood of Electrical Workers with the help of 17 Anning men in a six-month strike).[36]

Both S.I.S. and a big company called Universal Investigation Service Limited attempted to break the strike by Ottawa's private garbagemen in 1971. An S.I.S. guard who rode shotgun on a scab truck, Ron Wilson, claimed guards had been handed baseball bats—"two or three per truck"—before starting their collections. The company denied it.[37]

Argus Protection and Investigation Service of Windsor, Ontario, showed up during the strike in 1971 at Texpack Limited in Brantford. The company has since been taken over by Wackenhut of the United States.

S.I.S. also showed up in the 1971 Dominion Glass strike, the Kenroc strike in the same year, a strike at Canadian Longyear in 1970 at Thunder Bay, Ontario, Thermotex Windows in 1968 in Toronto and the 1964 strike-lockout in the three major Toronto daily newspapers involving the International Typographical Union.

Like Grange, the security companies tend to use manpower over-kill since the client pays the bill, writes it off taxable income as a business expense and hopes to eliminate the union. At Continental Can in 1969 in Toronto, Anning supplied 18 guards for a strike by 20 members of the Canadian Union of Operating Engineers who ran the boiler room.[38]

Anning had himself written up in a series of "case histories" he distributed as promotional literature a few years ago. One purports to be the story of a successfully broken strike ("Client: An Ontario Manufacturer"). Anning crows, "Clearly, the company's investment more than paid for itself by preventing property damage and helping to end a serious strike on terms favourable to management." Anning's director of marketing, a former Maclean-Hunter magazine advertising salesman named Ronald C. Harrington, shares his boss's enthusiasm for their work. "Our rates are competitive and the results outstanding," says Harrington.

The presence of the private security guard in labour disputes has been a feature of industrial relations almost since unions began in Canada and the United States. History reveals that the private guard is the catalyst of disorder, often under the direction of management. During a strike at the Adler and Sons Company in Milwaukee, Wisconsin, in 1928, a private detective from the Russell Detective Agency was seen driving a company car involved in a bombing. The detective, William Meese, tried to alter his testimony at a trial to determine responsibility for the bombing and was found guilty of criminal contempt.[39]

The first three decades of the century in the United States also saw mine guards convicted of kidnapping a strike leader, a union miner beaten to death by three mine guards in Pennsylvania, and detectives convicted of murder, manslaughter and attempted bribery.[40] Licensing the detective and guard agencies didn't stop anti-union violence. Even scab king Pearl Bergoff had a licence. When it was revoked by New York State authorities, Bergoff smugly announced, "I don't give a damn about the licence. I broke strikes for 17 years without any licence and I'll go on stronger than ever."[41] Most historians agree that Bergoff's professional strikebreaking business was bigger after he lost his licence than before.

New laws in the United States managed to do no more than dust off the business, not purge it. The La Follette committee of the U.S. Senate recommended private police be outlawed from labour disputes and called them "a menace to public peace". La Follette argued that since the private guards are accountable to no one but the company, unlike the public authorities, they are anti-democratic. "The use of private police as an agency of labour policy must be viewed, then, primarily as an attempt to impose upon labour a selfish, private interest by means of private armies." Their impact on industry was tremendous, in the committee's view. They give "unfair competitive advantage to those employers who oppress labour", they foment bitterness between workers and employers and actually "lead to strikes".[42]

The private police business and the professional strikebreaking racket, run with or without the security licence, are similar in motive: money, not peace.

The private police demand virtually full control of an assignment. It can become unclear just who is working for whom. In Montreal in 1966 the Citadel Investigation Agency Limited withdrew its guards from the harbour in a dispute with a stevedoring company that retained the company. "When we said six men were needed, they said only two," a Citadel spokesman complained. "Rather than operate that way, where the customer tells us how many men are necessary, we decided to get out."[43]

Citadel had a much more comfy arrangement five years before when the company worked for Upper Lakes Shipping Limited. The security agency was retained, explained Upper Lakes president John D. Leitch, because local police in port towns couldn't contain violence against the company's ships and crews. (A controversial membership raid was going on between the Seafarers' International Union of North America and the Canadian Maritime Union. S.I.U. strikes to force Upper Lakes to sign with the Seafarers' were blamed for several disturbances.) In 1961 and 1962 Leitch paid $361,000 to Citadel to guard his ships. No damage ever occurred while Citadel was on guard.[44]

A federal government commission to look into the S.I.U. and Upper Lakes was headed by T. G. Norris, a judge of the British Columbia Court of Appeal. S.I.U. lawyer Joseph Nuss charged during the hearings that the private police from Citadel had beaten Upper Lakes employees to frame S.I.U. members and discredit the union. Norris rejected the suggestion.

There were questions unanswered by the Norris commission about the role of Citadel and Upper Lakes Shipping in the S.I.U. uproar. Citadel's president, Leonard H. G. Speer, was also a partner in an obscure private investigation agency called Provincial Protection Bureau. Speer declared on August 7, 1962, in a statement under Quebec corporate-disclosure rules, that both Provincial and Citadel were operated out of the same Montreal office and from Speer's home in Ste. Foy, a suburb of Quebec City. Speer's partner in Provincial Protection Bureau was Bernard Merrigan of Montreal. Merrigan now lives in Toronto.

Merrigan was hired by Upper Lakes after the S.I.U. strike and is today its industrial-relations director and chief negotiator. Citadel had a less happy history. In 1970 the Quebec government revoked Speer's licence after the provincial police raided the agency's offices in the Mount Royal section of Montreal. There the police found electronic wiretapping equipment and phoney identification cards that let the holders pass themselves off as members of the Quebec Liquor Board police.[45]

Because of laws that prohibit the use of firearms by private police in Canada and the United States, one of the most vicious aspects of private-police activity has been erased. For some, the private police are at times too mild-mannered. A former strike-breaker for Rick Grange's Canadian Driver Pool says about Raymond Anning's operation: "Rick had very little respect for these people because they hired guards for $1.65 an hour, and at the first sign of trouble they'd take off—and who can blame them?"

Although the private guard agencies get big money from their clients, the men are low-paid, generally near the minimum wage ($1.65 an hour in 1972). It is not a salary that attracts a first-rate candidate. Recruits for the guard agencies are picked up literally right off the street and put into uniform. A former Anning operative says he got "absolutely no training". He was sent to the O.P.P. to apply for a licence and went to work right away.

Like professional strikebreakers, many security guards go into their line of work because they are unqualified for anything else. In a recent U.S. study, 40 per cent had been un-employed and said guard work was the best job they could get.

Only the most obviously unqualified are screened out. The quality of private police is probably no different in Canada than in the United States, where a recent study revealed that the business teems with corruption and sub-standard business practices. The study was conducted for the U.S. Department of Justice by the renowned Rand Corporation of Santa Monica, California. Rand found that 97 per cent of the guards questioned made "serious errors" about their own powers as private police "that could lead to civil suits or criminal charges". (Thirty-one per cent, for example, believe it's a crime for some-one to call them "pig".) Rand concluded "that substantial dishonesty and poor business practices exist" in the private-police business. Rand researchers guessed that there was probably a need for the private police and that crime rates would be higher without them. But Rand people were disturbed that executives of the guard business could offer no "qualitative evaluations" of their own worth.[46]

Governments and managements are so apprehensive that guards will organize collectively and turn against their bosses by refusing to do anti-labour work that tight laws have been passed keeping guards out of unions. In Ontario and elsewhere guards can't belong to unions that accept non-guards as members or affiliate to federations like the Canadian Labour Congress or the Confederation of National Trade Unions. The policy is pursued aggressively at all levels, it seems. Dudley Fletcher, a former organizer for the United Plant Guard Workers of America, says that, after he organized the private police force of Reliable Security Limited in Toronto, the company lost all its provincial government contracts. The work force dropped from 100 to 21 almost overnight, Fletcher claims. One contract was to guard the offices of the provincial Labour Department. Fletcher once took a crack at Raymond Anning's police, and one guard told him, "We can't be in a union."

The private police business would seem to be a natural domain for moonlighting city policemen. But in Metropolitan Toronto, at least, official department policy forbids it.

The department's policy states that the police are "expressly prohibited from engaging in any other business, employment or occupation. . . ." The reason naturally is so that the police appear, at least, to be impartial and not in the pay of anyone who could compromise an officer and affect his duties in serving the entire public.

Only what police call "pay duties" are permitted. These are privately paid but in general are in the same line as police work, such as directing traffic or patrolling large parties and other functions. Only occasionally does the policy lapse, as it did in 1970 during a strike by the International Brotherhood of Teamsters against three downtown Toronto fish-packing plants. The companies requested two officers for "pay duty" to watch picket lines. The same two officers assigned during the day were assigned in uniform to the night pay-duty. One, the son of Chief of Police Harold Adamson, said that there was no doubt in his mind that he could be impartial toward the strikers, even if he was in the pay of the company some of the time.

The danger of favouritism in such a situation was obvious to Deputy Police Chief Jack Ackroyd when a newspaper reporter asked him whether theoretically the police would let officers take pay-duty jobs for struck companies. ". . . I am sure a request for policemen to work pay duty at a strikebound plant would be turned down," Ackroyd responded.[47]

Such lapses of credibility are minor compared to how the police are seen in the eyes of unionists who have been on a picket line. One general complaint is that the police, whose salaries after all are paid by the strikers' taxes as well as the company's, are escorting strikebreakers through the picket line to take the strikers' jobs. Strikers complain that far too many police are used to guard picket lines and that the appearance of such excessive force is provocative and intimidating. Professional strikebreakers, too, get full police protection. How excessive the police strength can be is demonstrated in almost every industrial dispute. During a strike at Dominion Tape of Canada Limited in 1970 at Cornwall, Ontario, police sent 25 constables to protect a truck moving past 100 strikers. A police cruiser escorted the van as it sped away.[48] Twenty Ontario Provincial Police escorted the plant manager as he left for lunch during a strike at Motor Wheel Industries in Chatham, Ontario, in 1970. Eight cruisers watched a 10-man picket line that night.[49] In Plattsville, Ontario, in 1968, the O.P.P. confirmed it had provided six squad cars and between 20 and 24 men to guard a truck passing three women and two men on a picket line at the Canada Sand Papers Limited plant. Union estimates put the police at as many as 30 and the number of cruisers in the area at a dozen.[50] The following year the O.P.P. formed a flying wedge of 80 men to smash through a picket line to allow trucks to pass 25 strikers who had sat down in front of the plant gates at SKD Manufacturing Company in Amherstburg.[51] In the same year, 60 city policemen in Brantford, backed up by 11 O.P.P. officers, overpowered strikers to help strikebreakers leave Chicago Rawhide Products Canada Limited during a United Auto Workers' strike. Twenty policemen watched 25 picketers afterwards.[52]

Using police to keep plants going has come to be considered essential by anti-union managements. One manufacturer, Northern Gilbro Manufacturing Limited, advertised in *The Windsor Star* for scabs in 1970 and told applicants in the ad that they would receive police protection. (The advertised starting rate was higher than the striking employees had been paid.)[53] There is no record in Canada of strikers ever demanding that it is equally *the strikers'* privilege to call the police to prevent strikebreakers from stealing the employees' jobs.

Anti-strikebreaking laws in the United States and other countries really do require the police to eject, not help the professional scab. In Canton, Ohio, in early 1972, city police removed 20 strikebreakers from the printing plant of the town's only daily newspaper. Canton is one of more than 115 U.S. cities that outlaw professional strikebreaking. Courts in Chile have upheld the right of striking employees to file complaints with the police and demand that strikebreakers be evicted from the plants and offices during disputes.

(Although Ontario government ministers claim the technical definition of a professional strikebreaker is difficult to ascertain, several American states and scores of cities have had no trouble. Most define the professional strikebreaker as "any person who customarily and repeatedly offers himself for employment in the place of employees involved" in a labour-management dispute. A standard legal definition of "customarily and repeatedly" is twice. Such laws obviously would stop professional strikebreaking in Ontario, where Driver Pool personnel and others often take the jobs of striking truck drivers and warehouse personnel. Typical penalties in the U.S. range from fines of $25 to $500 and six-month prison terms (in San Francisco) up to maximum fines of $1,000 and one-year jail terms (in the state of Pennsylvania and the city of New York). John J. Pilch, president of the International Typographical Union and a leading anti-professional strikebreaking campaigner, says the U.S. laws are effective. ". . . There has not been a single instance of a strikebreaker-prolonged strike" where anti-strikebreaking laws exist, Pilch wrote the Labour Council of Metropolitan Toronto in April, 1972. The I.T.U. has a list of endorsements for anti-strikebreaking laws from governors, mayors and state labour and trade officials, who say typically that such laws have had no detrimental impact on the ability to attract new industries.)

Occasionally the police have more than obliged the employer by not only guarding scabs but even scabbing themselves. During the 1970 Motor Wheel Industries strike in Chatham, 19 members of the O.P.P. cleaned up garbage that strikers had piled in front of the main entrance before whisking the plant manager and the personnel director past the line.[54]

In 1972, during the lengthy Dare Foods Limited strike in Kitchener, city police were sent out of town to meet a convoy of Driver Pool-driven trucks headed toward the struck plant. A crash involving four trucks and a police cruiser resulted as the police stopped to try to censor a radio reporter in his own car who was about to broadcast the convoy's arrival. Kitchener chief Wilfred Henrich, when asked why the city police felt it was their right to leave their jurisdiction to escort the strikebreakers, replied to a newspaperman, "Under the Police Act we have the power to go anywhere in the performance of duty."

Obviously the police departments of Ontario are being used by employers to move non-critical shipments (or empty trucks) and escort temporary replacements, in order to gain a bargaining advantage over the union. During the 1971 strike at Kimberly-Clark of Canada Limited in St. Catharines, Ontario,

35 to 50 policemen continually showed up, as the union put it in a leaflet, "to insure that the union's legal picket line did not interfere with the transport of fancy toilet tissues in and out of the mill". Testifying at the trial of Richard Grange and the Metro policeman, Barry Chapman, a Kimberly-Clark executive said that the plant did not produce at all during the six-month strike that ended in early 1972. There was then the following exchange between prosecutor Frank Armstrong and the executive, Edward J. Brady:

ARMSTRONG: As a matter of economics, how was it that you were able to exist under the situation?

BRADY: Well, this is only one plant that we have, and business at the present moment is in a recession, so product was really no problem.

ARMSTRONG: You didn't have to move product out of St. Catharines?

BRADY: Not to supply our customers.[55]

Although management expects during a strike that the police will serve and protect them, not the company's employees, it's the community at large that pays ultimately. Police officials and public authorities rarely speak out about the cost of police services to companies in strikes. But the costs are large. At the current rate for first-class constables in Metropolitan Toronto, the community pays $5.60 an hour for policemen ($8.40 an hour for overtime) when officers are assigned to strike duty. It is a waste of manpower because, while the police are preventing or mopping up after incidents provoked by companies and professional strikebreakers, other parts of the community are not served and protected. The monetary loss may be incalculable. But an estimate of how professional strikebreakers are causing police administration budgets to soar can be extrapolated from the figures that the chief of police of Kitchener gave for a 1971 strike that lasted only seven days at Raymond Snack Foods Limited. It cost the department and the taxpayers of Kitchener more than $6,000 in overtime and stand-by pay.[56]

Not only do companies expect the police to help defeat the union—and expect the public to pay for it—so do the professional strikebreakers. One strikebreaker, at the preliminary hearing for the Grange trial in 1971, said "the police were always present for our own protection".[57]

Some police forces actually go out of their way to help the professional strikebreakers. It is common practice for strikers to trail trucks to their destination and try to persuade the workers or companies on the receiving end to cut off orders from the struck plant until the walkout is over. During a strike by the United Auto Workers at Smith & Stone Canada Limited in Georgetown, Ontario, in 1971, strikers followed a truck driven by professional strikebreakers. Their car was ordered off the road by an O.P.P. cruiser. An officer warned the strikers that the car had a thin tire, says Harry Dewhurst, an official of the U.A.W. local. "The cops were obviously tipped off," says Dewhurst. He wondered, recalling the incident later, the last time an O.P.P. cruiser routinely stopped a car for a bald tire.

A similar incident occurred during the Canada Sand Papers strike in Plattsville, where members of the International Chemical Workers' Union were on strike. Strikers tailed a truck—guarded by 20 O.P.P. officers, according to one newspaper report—and their car was stopped by an O.P.P. officer who just wanted to know if the driver had a licence. The scab-cargo truck got away.[58]

Unionists find it hard to reconcile the pay and status of the average policeman, who is a public servant, with the outright aid that the police give managements in labour disputes. There are many theories to explain this situation. The police officer is, first of all, a member of the public bombarded with the same prejudiced anti-union messages as everyone else. And even if an individual policeman is sympathetic, he is only following orders. The bias of the police establishment is in favour of law and order and against the demonstrator, who is seen as the cause, not the victim, of turmoil at the picket line.

A revealing letter was sent to the Labour Council of Metropolitan Toronto in 1972 by the deputy chief of police for field operations of the Metro Toronto police department. He stated, "On many occasions the police are not required to be at strike locations as the conduct of the pickets does not warrant police attention."[59] That the conduct of the employer or his mercenaries, the professional strikebreakers, could ever need the attention of the police apparently never occurred to the police administration.

Picket-line disturbances always work to the disadvantage of the union. Although the police may not understand that simple fact, the professional strikebreaker does. At a strike where Canadian Driver Pool supplied trucks and drivers for Pioneer Electric in Toronto, says a former Driver Pool strikebreaker, a company official tried to manufacture incidents so the police would have an excuse to come down hard on the union members. "The company tried to get the trucks to run through the picket lines at the times of heaviest concentration so they could lay charges," says the strikebreaker.

Only recently has public attention been focused on the morale and fitness of the men and women in police uniforms. The first solid research is not encouraging. The police system itself breeds conflict between strikers and policemen. The men on patrol may have been passed over for promotions. Many probably hate strike work. "Inevitably, the patrol officers are not the men thought of within the department as being the best . . .," says Paul Jacobs, an American sociologist.[60] Although government, management and academics all recognize labour relations as a special kind of dynamic in society, the police receive no training or education in unionism and labour law that might give them insights into the values and motives of striking workers. According to Jack Ackroyd, Toronto's deputy chief, "Generally the men assigned [to strike duties] are not specifically trained in strike duty but are trained in the law and how it applies to the public in general, which is all that is necessary."[61]

Strike-duty procedures spelled out in the Metro department's regulations do say specifically that officers should "keep an absolutely impartial attitude—be firm and courteous". Another rule directs officials not to "fraternize with either pickets or management or express opinions". The regulations, if followed to the letter, also allow the police to make the law, not just enforce it. One regulation orders "NO MASS PICKETING". Although mass picketing is legal (unless stifled by a court injunction), the Toronto police regulations state that "no more than four" pickets "would usually be required at each entrance". Police officers are instructed, in effect, to make their own injunctions.

There appears to be no published research on what the police think of strike work. But policemen, predictably, like exciting jobs more than the routine. In a survey of one large American city's police department, "catching a burglar at work" and other crime-busting duties far out-scored the tedious but more common police work of issuing traffic tickets, checking hazards, going to "domestic" calls and checking the homes of people on vacation.[62]

In a way the police are the victims, too, of the government's casual refusal to face up to the growth of a criminal element in professional strikebreaking and the potential for violent confrontation in that element. Like doctors facing the question of whether to perform an abortion, the policeman is likewise stuck with decisions on the picket line that government hasn't had the courage to make. The police are frequently under criticism for enforcing laws that are obsolete or for dealing too ruggedly with civilians.

For a variety of reasons, the police are not as popular as they used to be with the law-abiding public they protect. In the most recent Gallup Poll of Canada (1969), almost one-quarter of the population nationwide said that they would hesitate to say that generally they approve of the way the police work. Although praise was highest in Ontario of any province, so was the amount of criticism (13 per cent in the province stated unequivocally that they "disapproved").[63]

Training is the root of police improvement, says the Canadian Civil Liberties Association. "It is common knowledge that police work often attracts candidates with severe emotional problems," the association told then-Attorney-General Arthur Wishart in 1969. "To such people, the duties of a police officer afford an opportunity to vent their hostilities with the sanction of uniform and law. Every police force, no matter how admirable its record, has such misfits on its roster."

The association says that what's needed to sensitize the police is "a shift in emphasis from brawn to brain". The C.C.L.A. observed, "There appears to be very little emphasis on human rights and civil liberties issues."

Which side are the police on? "I think the average policeman puts himself in the position of the average working man," says Syd Brown, president of the 5,000-member Metropolitan Toronto Police Association. Brown's position is, "I'm opposed to policemen being used at all in strike situations. If the company weren't allowed to operate, there wouldn't be any need for a picket line. . . . It's my firm belief if there's a legal strike the company should shut down. The police or anybody else shouldn't get involved." Brown claims his view is that of the majority of his members.

Strike duty may be unpleasant, but it is money. Zealous Toronto police constables even reported early to patrol the Gidon Industries strike with Canadian Driver Pool in 1972, stopping off on their way to work and racking up extra overtime. It's hard for many unionists to reconcile a good deal of police belligerence in strikes with the unionizing of policemen themselves. Although Brown and other police leaders adamantly deny that their associations are unions or want to be or associate with unions, they are labour organizations. In the United States some police associations are affiliating with the American Federation of Labour and Congress of Industrial Organizations.

Two industrial-relations specialists in the United States who studied 214 police organizations in the late 1960's say "most of these organizations function as unions regardless of their affiliations".[64] When police organizations first sprouted in the early part of the century in the United States and the United Kingdom, there was fear in city halls "that the police would side with the class from which most of them came, against the middle classes".[65] Most objective scholars agree that police unions are good, for the police and the public. "Since police unions will also contribute to the civilian character of the police, their growth should be encouraged," says one. The public, he says, "should do everything we can to encourage" affiliation of police organizations with the mainstream labour movement since the A.F.L.-C.I.O. "remains a bulwark of our [U.S.] democracy".[66] Another police expert says, "Where police unions have taken root in America, they appear to have a democratizing effect." This man quotes the chief of police in Boston, who says, "The union reduced authoritarianism" in the department.[67] The author of *Upgrading the American Police* says, however, "Police unions, growing in power and increasingly aggressive in their demands for better salaries, have never been known as ardent advocates of better training."[68] Only a few thousand of about a quarter of a million American policemen are in unions, and only a handful are in this country. But the police union movement is strong in Sweden, where the 13,000-member Swedish Union of Policemen is the fourteenth biggest union in the country.[69] If the public or civic officials feel that a unionized police force would be partial towards other unions, they should not worry, says U.S. mediator Theodore W. Kheel. He notes that the same impartiality issue was also raised when newspaper reporters began to organize. Publishers argued that their reporters and editors would slant news in favour of the labour movement. Kheel thinks the publishers were wrong.[70]

If strikers believe the police are too friendly with professional strikebreakers, it's a suspicion given new justification by the arrest and conviction of police constable Barry Chapman with Richard Grange in 1971. Unionists assume the police work closely with professional strikebreakers. They are more right than they think.

The suspicion grows with the knowledge that so many policemen leave police work for private detective agencies. The three Ontario guard companies bought out and merged by American guard mogul George Wackenhut in 1971 were all headed by ex-policemen: Raymond Anning, John Forrest of

Argus and Robert Cullen (Trans-Canada Protection Services).[71] Syd Brown of the Toronto police association says "several hundred" have quit the force in the past several years to work for security firms.

Despite Brown's claim that most police officers identify with the working class, it's difficult for strikers not to believe that the average policeman is more typified by Rick Grange's long-time friend, Kevin McEwan. It was natural that one day Grange and McEwan would go into business together. They double-dated. They threw stag parties for one another when each got married. "You know," McEwan told a reporter after he joined Grange's strikebreaking operation, "there's a future in this business and a lot of money to be made in it." Young (he was 25 when he joined the Grange gang) and ambitious, McEwan hated traffic work. His brief tour as a plainclothesman was far more fun. Driver Pool and strike work were exciting. "I learned more in two months with Canadian Driver Pool than in three years on the police force," he says. His attitudes (and his factual information) about unions are not much different from those of other professional strikebreakers. For a policeman, though, his outlook on the assortment of known hoodlums and strong-arm men hired by Grange might be unusual. "I don't see anything wrong with hiring guys who have records," he told an acquaintance in April, 1972. (McEwan's nonchalance about whom he worked with is reminiscent of the remark of James B. Waddell, a partner in the U.S. strikebreaking giant, Pearl Bergoff. Waddell told the U.S. Senate anti-strikebreaking investigation "he has no prejudice against ex-convicts, but, on the contrary, finds many of them particularly valuable for the work on hand".)[72]

Grange confidently tells employers who hire him, in his manual for operating during a strike, that the "police strike squad" has been alerted and that "patrol cars from our division will visit the plant several times during the hours of darkness. . . ." Grange also pledges that "the strike squad will be on duty during the day".

Technically, the Toronto police department's strike squad was merged in late 1971 with the intelligence division. According to Deputy Police Chief Jack Ackroyd there is no "special squad assigned to strike duty exclusively". Grange's manual lists the names of four persons identified as policemen, including strike-squad head Stuart Kennedy. Other police named with their telephone numbers are Sergeant Harold Crowe, Kennedy's assistant; Inspector Redbirth Spurling, who never was with the strike squad; and George Day. Spurling is head of the summons branch. He has an office in downtown Toronto on Richmond Street East in the same building as the intelligence branch and the members of the old "strike squad". Day is a civilian who assists Kennedy.

Grange has obtained, apparently from officers on the force, the confidential telephone numbers for nighttime checks on criminal records and licence plates. It is against the rules of the department and the Ontario Police Act to divulge such departmental secrets.

Grange stays on the good side of the police in other ways. One employee who has left the organization says Grange tips the police on suspicious activity. He informed the police about a gambling operation one day, a former associate says, and also told the gamblers, who cleared out before the police arrived.

Grange often bragged to his troops that the Toronto police emergency task force "was at his disposal", a former strikebreaker remembers. The task force, explains Deputy Chief Ackroyd, is specially trained in crowd control and is used against picketers when they show too much "militancy".[73] For a time it appeared that an entire cell in the department supported Driver Pool. Both McEwan and ex-cop Barry Dantzic, who worked for Grange for a while, came out of Division 3 in the northwest end of Metropolitan Toronto. So did Barry Chapman, who was convicted with Grange in the wiretap-conspiracy trial.

Former employees say Grange hands photographs of strikers and other tidbits he picks up about unions to Stu Kennedy, head of the intelligence branch section of the Toronto police, which used to be the strike squad. Kennedy is a familiar figure to unionists. "The unions trust me," he proudly tells acquaintances. In exchange Kennedy provided Grange with information the police knew about individuals on picket lines. When Grange felt there weren't enough police around to guard his strikebreakers and his trucks, he would call Stu Kennedy "personally", says a one-time Grange cohort.

According to Syd Brown of the police association, the strike squad also gives information to management about employees who act up on picket lines. This information from police informants can be used by management to take reprisals against strikers up to and including dismissal.

What Grange's intimate dealings with the police mean is simply the use of public law-enforcement officers for private and profit motives. This practice undermines confidence in the force on the part of the public, which includes a sizeable number of unionists. A lack of faith in the integrity of the police makes the job of the policeman tougher. Judge Garth Moore raised the issue of police corruption when sentencing Grange and Chapman in April, 1972, for the wiretapping conviction. Judge Moore said Grange had found in Chapman "a policeman who was willing to be corrupted". If the police deal directly as partners with a strikebreaking agency that could be a front for organized crime, the possibility of other types of corruption goes up.

Corruption of the police is a threat to the democratic system, not merely to the jobs of some strikers. "It is quite evident that corruption has been a part of many if not all totalitarian police systems," relates George Berkley, a leading authority on police administration. "Corruption induces its beneficiaries to act arbitrarily, while it secures for its perpetrators unequal and favourable treatment. It debases all parties to its acts and opens the door to many tendencies that are antithetical to democracy such as secrecy, self-contempt, and disregard for all law."[74]

Backing up an anti-union police are the anti-union courts, whose decisions also have helped spread professional strikebreaking. The traditional antipathy between the judicial system and the labour movement is evident from the downpouring of injunctions and other court decisions that have gone against the labour movement (see Chapter 2). Unions are understandably wary of the courts. David Archer, president of the Ontario Federation of Labour, explains why. "Most judges neither have the expertise nor the sympathy to understand industrial relations," he says. "The farther we stay away from the courts, the better off we are."[75] The courts have been used frequently by employers to defeat unions. Anti-picketing injunctions have made the court system contemptible in the eyes of many unionists. A. Alan Borovoy, general counsel for the Canadian Civil Liberties Association, believes judges refuse to understand the purpose of picketing or the nature of the struggle the picket line represents. A "legitimate objective" of picketing, Borovoy asserts, is "to exert social pressure on those who would violate the picket line, the so-called scab. The pickets can't hope to persuade, rationally, people to obey their cause or to adhere to their cause. The best thing they can do is to make the picket line violator as socially uncomfortable as they can. I'm not talking about inflicting violence or physically obstructing people," continues Borovoy, "clearly pickets are not allowed to do that. But they should be entitled to visit their collective contempt and social disapproval on those who would violate their picket line."[76]

Even far down the line in the judicial system the courts help the professional strikebreaker. The courts are used, at great cost in administrative expenses to the taxpayers, by professional strikebreakers to intimidate striking employees. They are used in the strikebreakers' strategy of laying wholesale charges against picketers. The inconvenience and harassment this means for the striking employees is obvious.

In most big city "industrial ghetto" strikes, where a preponderance of the strikers are recent immigrants, mischievous phoney charges raise the fear that the immigrant may be deported or not get citizenship because he or she has a police record. Unfamiliar with Canadian customs, the language or the courts, the immigrant can easily be frightened off the picket line by a strikebreaker's intentionally unfounded charge. During the Kenroc Tools strike, Driver Pool thugs and the police laid various charges for alleged common assault, damage and "creating a public nuisance". All but one of the 12 strikers charged were acquitted. The lone charge that stuck was for causing damage under $50. The fine was $100.

Most of the charges laid during strikes are dismissed, usually for lack of evidence and as often because the strikebreakers or the police who lay them do not show up when the striker appears in court. The defendant loses a day's pay. Richard Grange claimed in late 1971 that in two years his strikebusters had laid 384 charges against strikers. He said he kept no record of how many led to convictions. Former employees say Grange's claim is ridiculous, but they admit that charges were laid against strikers as part of the strikebreaking strategy. The laying of unfounded charges could be grounds for another charge—of mischief and creating a public nuisance against the professional strikebreakers.

Professional strikebreakers also fail to show in court for charges laid against them. A Driver Pool man charged with possession of a dangerous weapon failed to show up to face the charge in Oakville, Ontario, in 1972. A warrant was issued for his arrest.

A striker who went to court to face a charge laid by a professional strikebreaker during the AP Parts strike in 1971 was sent home and the charge dropped when the plaintiff failed to show up. One reason the strikebreaker may have failed to show, says lawyer Clayton Peterson, the union counsel, is that police told him the strikebreaker was a wanted man and probably feared detection in the halls of justice.

"We have laid hundreds of charges against union members," Grange proudly told a newspaper in 1971, "but we've never had one against us."[77] His statement that no charges had been laid against Driver Pool was a lie. But on balance many more charges have been laid against unionists. The reason isn't, as it would seem at first glance, more lawlessness on the side of the strikers. Unionists have tried to lay charges against Driver Pool lawbreakers, but it isn't easy. Douglas Hart, a representative of the United Steelworkers of America, found this out. A band of Driver Pool thugs ambushed the Steelworkers' trailer used as a strike headquarters during a walkout in early 1972 at Central Precision Limited in northwestern Metropolitan Toronto. Hart suspected trouble from Driver Pool thugs, and kept three strikers asleep inside the trailer at night. They saw and identified some of the attackers. But when Hart went to swear out charges, the Justice of the Peace refused to take the information and issue summonses unless Hart had the names and addresses of all the alleged perpetrators. The justice of the peace told him this, says Hart, although scores of charges are laid against unionists and others every year on the basis of crimes committed by suspects identified and "persons unknown". Although the trailer attack and a fire-bombing the same night of the car belonging to the president of the striking local union both were reported right away to the police, Division 23 officers claimed they had no record of the incidents when Hart went to them to substantiate his story before the Justice of the Peace.

Justices of the Peace do have discretion in issuing a summons to appear in court on charges, or a warrant for a suspect's arrest. But this discretion has been used sparingly against professional strikebreakers. The J.P.'s duties are clearly spelled out in the federal Criminal Code. The Justice of the Peace must hear and consider the allegations of the informant who wants to lay the charge and ponder the evidence of witnesses, where he thinks it's desirable. "Too often," said J. C. McRuer in his findings for the Ontario Royal Commission on Civil Rights, issuing a summons or a warrant "is treated as a mere formality" by a J.P. "More frequently than not," McRuer found, "when the police officer asks for a warrant he gets one without demonstrating the need for it."[78]

Bail is also granted arbitrarily. Doug Hart of the Steelworkers was charged with assault for allegedly spitting at a scab's car during the long strike Grange worked at Gidon Industries

Limited in suburban Toronto. As a condition of bail, Hart was banished from the picket line. The effect on the strikers' morale was bad, Hart says. But none of three Driver Pool men charged with more serious crimes at Gidon was banished from the picket line as a condition of bail. (When Hart appeared in court, the police withdrew the charge.)

The complicity of the government, the courts, the police and other authorities in power is mandatory for professional strikebreaking to flourish. It is the stated public policy of the government of Ontario, in the preamble to the Labour Relations Act, that "it is in the public interest . . . to further harmonious relations between employers and employees by encouraging the practice and procedure of collective bargaining. . . ." Since that is provincial policy, the many levels of authority in Ontario that aid professional strikebreakers in their campaign to promote turbulence for profit are not only hypocrites, but quite possibly lawbreakers. The rights of workers to organize to better their standard of living is supposed to be protected by law. But the real weight of enforcement is not on the workers' side, it is on the side of the entrenched and powerful ownership class. So far society has tolerated the stacking of government power in favour of the professional strikebreakers like Canadian Driver Pool.

Perhaps someday public attitudes will change and people will see that the police, the various ministers of the provincial cabinet, and the courts "must be geared not only to catch the crooks", as the Canadian Civil Liberties Association once said, "but also to protect our rights".

Notes

1. Brooks, R. R. R., *When Labour Organizes*, Yale University Press, New Haven, Conn., 1937, cited in Taylor and Witney, *op. cit.*, p. 131.
2. *An Almanac of Liberty*, Doubleday, New York, 1954, p. 355.
3. *Fortune, op. cit.*, p. 89.
4. *Regina v. Dobias*, Ontario Reports, 1972, Volume 1, (Essex County Court), pp. 226-227.
5. *Hansard*, April 6, 1972, p. 868.
6. *The* (Toronto) *Telegram*, June 15, 1971..
7. *Regina vs. Barry Chapman and Richard Grange*, (Preliminary hearing transcript) *op. cit.*, p. 115.
8. *Regina vs. Barry Chapman and Richard Grange*, (Trial transcript), *op. cit.*, p. 224.
9. *Ibid.*, p. 265.
10. *Ibid.*, p. 271.

11. *Ibid.*
12. *The* (Toronto) *Telegram,* June 18, 1971.
13. *Ibid.*
14. *The Globe and Mail,* December 15, 1971.
15. *The* (Toronto) *Telegram,* June 15, 1971.
16. *Toronto Star,* October, 1971.
17. *The Globe and Mail,* December 15, 1971.
18. Letter of December 20, 1971.
19. *Hansard,* December 14, 1971, p. 50.
20. *Hansard,* May 1, 1972, p. 1838.
21. *The* (Toronto) *Telegram,* October 15, 1971.
22. *The* (Brantford, Ontario) *Expositor,* September 17, 1971.
23. *The Globe and Mail,* October 13, 1971.
24. *The Globe and Mail,* October 15, 1971.
25. *The London* (Ontario) *Evening Free Press,* September 17, 1971.
26. *The Globe and Mail,* January 8, 1972.
27. *Toronto Daily Star,* June 10, 1970.
28. *The Globe and Mail,* September 23, 1970.
29. Justin, Brother Cornelius, F. S. C.; Hays, Paul R., and Isaacson, William J., *Report of the Special Committee of Investigation to Industrial Commissioner Catherwood,* State of New York Department of Labour, Albany, N.Y., 1959, p. 30.
30. *Ibid.*
31. *The* (Toronto) *Telegram,* August 28, 1971.
32. "We Never Sleep," *Newsweek,* July 31, 1961, p. 64; "The Super Sleuths," *Newsweek,* August 31, 1959, p. 67; "Junior Burns Man," *Newsweek,* May 22, 1961, p. 60.
33. "Last of Pinkertons Keeps Watch," *Business Week,* March 5. 1960, p. 79.
34. *Hansard,* April 7, 1972. p. 947.
35. *The* (Toronto) *Telegram,* October 28, 1969.
36. Rinehart, James W., "A Strike That Failed," *Canadian Dimension,* March-April, 1972, p. 6.
37. *The Ottawa Citizen,* August 12, 1971, p. 37.
38. *The Globe and Mail,* January 18, 1969.
39. *State v. Meese,* 200 Wis. 454, 225 N. W. 746 (1929).
40. *University of Pennsylvania Law Review, op. cit.,* p. 407 (footnote).
41. Wolf, *op. cit.,* p. 569.
42. Cited in Auerbach, *op. cit.,* pp. 267, 272.
43. Canadian Press report carried in *The Globe and Mail,* November 16, 1966.
44. Norris, R. G. *Report of Industrial Inquiry Commission on the Disruption of Shipping,* Queen's Printer, Ottawa, 1963, pp. 82-84.
45. Canadian Press report carried in *The Globe and Mail,* October 2, 1970.
46. *The New York Times,* April 9, 1972, p. 58.
47. *The* (Toronto) *Telegram,* June 12, 1970.
48. *The Ottawa Citizen,* March 7, 1970.
49. *The Globe and Mail,* June 12, 1970.
50. *The Windsor* (Ontario) *Star,* March 18, 1968.
51. *Toronto Daily Star,* August 13, 1969.
52. *The* (Brantford, Ontario) *Expositor,* March 14, 1969.
53. *The Windsor* (Ontario) *Star,* August 7, 1970.
54. *The London* (Ontario) *Evening Free Press,* June 10, 1970.

55. Trial transcript, *op. cit.,* p. 270.
56. *The Kitchener-Waterloo* (Ontario) *Record,* May 18, 1971.
57. Preliminary hearing transcript, *op. cit.,* p. 110.
58. *The Windsor* (Ontario) *Star,* March 18, 1968.
59. Letter to Laurel MacDowell, research coordinator, Labour Council of Metropolitan Toronto, from J. W. Ackroyd, May 19, 1972.
60. Jacobs, Paul, *Prelude to Riots: A View of Urban America from the Bottom,* Random House, New York, 1966, p. 56.
61. Ackroyd, *op. cit.*
62. Olson, Bruce, "An Explanatory Study of Task Preferences," *Personnel Journal,* December, 1970.
63. Source: The Canadian Institute of Public Opinion, Toronto.
64. Juris, Harvey, A. and Hutchison, Kay B., "The Legal Status of Municipal Police Employee Organizations," *Industrial and Labour Relations Review.* Vol. 23, No. 3, Cornell University, April, 1970, p. 362.
65. Martin, J. P. and Wilson, Gail, *The Police: A Study in Manpower,* Heinneman, London, England, 1969, p. 63.
66. Berkley, George E., *The Democratic Policeman,* Beacon Press, Boston, Massachusetts, 1969, p. 203.
67. *Ibid.,* p. 52.
68. Saunders, Charles B. Jr., *Upgrading the American Police,* The Brookings Institute, Washington, D. C., 1970, p. 145.
69. Schuster, *op. cit.,* From tables on pp. 396, 398.
70. *American Labour,* September, 1969, p. 55.
71. Burgess, Drummond, "Strikebreakers, Inc.," *Last Post,* November, 1971, pp. 33-36.
72. Levinson, *op. cit.,* p. 724.
73. Ackroyd letter, *op. cit.*
74. Berkley, *op. cit.,* pp. 124-125.
75. *The Globe and Mail,* October 8, 1971, p. 3.
76. *Ibid.*
77. *The* (Toronto) *Telegram,* June 12, 1971.
78. McRuer, J. C., *Royal Commission Inquiry into Civil Rights,* Report No. 1, Vol. 2, Queen's Printer, Toronto, 1968, p. 739.

6

Today Ontario,
Tomorrow. . .

"The American worker doesn't yet believe in the class struggle, but the American employer has been Marxist for generations."

Dwight MacDonald, reporting on the La Follette committee hearings in The Nation, *February 27, 1937*

Besides the official help in high circles given Richard Grange and other professional strikebreaking forces in Ontario, there is a surfeit of help from other friends. Individuals from groups as diverse as the legal profession and the religious community* have helped strikebreakers commit their assaults on the union movement. Special interest groups, like the Canadian Manufacturers' Association and the mass media, are more dependable sources of support for professional strikebreakers.

*Normally religious leaders don't get involved in secular matters like strikes and lockouts. But there have been exceptions. In 1969 the International Union of Electrical Workers went on strike against U.S.-owned Proctor-Silex Limited in Picton, Ontario. The Reverend Robert Stewart of the St. Mary Magdalene Anglican Church claimed the union's chief negotiator had used "Mafia tactics". "When actions like these occur, it is time for Picton to say that the Mafia get out of Picton and return to Italy," according to newspaper reports. What provoked the minister's wrath was the presence of I.U.E. representative James Donofrio, an Italian-Canadian organizer. The company (now called Proctor-Lewyt) broke the union. In 1971 when the workers at Toronto's Irwin Toy Limited were preparing to strike for a first agreement, an influential priest from the Portuguese community visited the plant and talked many of the immigrants out of supporting the strike, according to a union organizer. Most earned the minimum wage. About half the plant's 150 workers supported the strike, which dragged on from August, 1971, to June the following year.

Management lawyers who act as advisers on labour matters refer their clients to professional strikebreakers like Anning Investigations Limited and Canadian Driver Pool. When the law firm is particularly well-connected, like Grange's, a good word in the right place means more business for Driver Pool.

Grange's legal advisers are from the law firm of Gardiner and Roberts. The Gardiner in the firm is Fred Gardiner, the former chairman of the Corporation of Metropolitan Toronto whose political friends gave him the nickname "Big Daddy".

The involvement of the Canadian Manufacturers' Association in professional strikebreaking is hardly surprising. The C.M.A. is an organization of 7,700 businesses. Consistently since the group's founding more than 100 years ago, C.M.A. leaders have gushed anti-union propaganda like a geyser. They have lobbied governments for firmer controls on unions and truculently attacked the labour movement from any platform available to them (see Chapter 2).

In its own words, the C.M.A. conducts "extensive publicity and public relations activity . . . throughout the year . . ."[1] Much of the publicity is anti-labour. Typical of the association's reactionary postures on industrial relations was the unsuccessful lobby in 1970 to make the federal Department of Labour and the National Film Board of Canada suppress a film about the impact of automation on white-collar workers. The C.M.A. summarized the colour movie adequately. "It is a fictionalized motion picture describing the installation of a computer and the subsequent heartless displacement of a large number of employees from the company concerned." The C.M.A., believing that such "heartless" actions never occur in the name of profits, protested to the Labour Department that the film "not only failed to achieve objectivity, but cast employers in a most unfair light".[2] The deputy minister of labour, J. Douglas Love, replied that withdrawing the film from circulation "would not be justified".

It was probably inevitable that the C.M.A. and Richard Grange of Canadian Driver Pool would develop a relationship. Grange is probably the only professional strikebreaker to supply services to two C.M.A. presidents. In 1970 Driver Pool got its first major assignment during the strike by the United Auto Workers at Honeywell Controls Limited in Scarborough, Ontario. Honeywell's president at the time, the late Leonard F. Wills, was also C.M.A. president during the same year. Wills conveniently forgot to mention the strike at his own plant while he was reminding industrialists like himself that they have a patriotic duty to force unions to restrain their contract goals. In one typical speech he said businessmen have got to get tough with unions and added, "We in industry have the right to expect the full backing of the authority of government."[3] U.A.W. strikers took up the theme and paraded with picket signs reading "On Strike Against the C.M.A.", while Canadian Driver Pool dashed across their picket lines.

The year after the Honeywell strike, Grange got a lot of business from another C.M.A. president, A. G. W. Sinclair, president of Canadian Johns-Manville. (Johns-Manville is one of the most violent strikes in Driver Pool's record. A Driver Pool thug threatened to beat up a Manville worker not involved in the strike who stopped one day to take photographs of the strikebreakers. Billyclubs and baseball bats wielded by Driver Pool heavies were confiscated by the police, according to former Driver Pool men. On more than one occasion, says Jim Taylor, president of Local 346 of the International Chemical Workers' Union, the cars of union members tailing Driver Pool trucks were forced off the roads by strikebreakers, who tried to get the strikers to fight.

The C.M.A. has not only a reactionary record when it comes to industrial relations, but also an inconsistent one. For years C.M.A. lobbyists have pushed for more stringent legislative straitjackets on the growth of unions. Naturally the C.M.A.'s favourite theme is law and order. When mass picketing broke stronghold injunctions in 1966 at *The Oshawa Times* newspaper and at the Tilco Plastics Limited strike in Peterborough, the C.M.A.'s reaction was Pavlovian. "The worst part of the whole business, of course," said H. B. Style, the C.M.A. president, "is that the law of the land can be defied this way."[4] He was even more militant later that year, saying, "It appears more and more that some elements of labour are prepared to ruin the nation in order to establish supremacy of their authority."[5]

On the other hand, since the C.M.A. has been so law-and-order-prone over the years, it seems unusual that the association would welcome into its arms the president of Canadian Driver Pool, a man with a criminal record who heads a company specializing in violence and employing convicted lawbreakers.

But the contradiction is only apparent. The involvement of the C.M.A. in strikebreaking goes back a long time. Historian Charles Lipton says that in the early years of the century, the C.M.A. was "heavily involved" in recruiting immigrants from Asia and the British Isles to serve as strikebreakers.[6]

Richard Grange apparently got deeply involved with the

C.M.A. in 1971 when Driver Pool inserted itself into the strike at Trane Company of Canada Limited. Trane vice-president Fred B. Symmes, a C.M.A. activist, got excited about the idea of a strikebreaking army on stand-by at all times at the call of managements. Grange impressed him. With that foot in the door, Grange met William H. Wightman, manager of the industrial relations department at the C.M.A.'s downtown Toronto headquarters and a management representative on the Ontario Labour Relations Board, which administers the province's bargaining and organizing laws. Grange met Wightman at the C.M.A. offices several times. When Grange's sales letters to executives offering to break their companies' strikes were divulged in the Legislature, the C.M.A. wrote Grange a letter of endorsement, former employees recall. One says that the letter told Grange the C.M.A. was "behind him 100 per cent". His operation was beneficial to industry because Grange's presence would deter strikes before they start. Wightman apparently made big plans for Grange. He took him to Vancouver for a speaking engagement. Former strikebreakers say the C.M.A. planned to take Grange on a nationwide speaking tour, though it never materialized. Some say Grange's arrest for the Redpath Sugars Limited wiretap in October, 1971, temporarily interrupted the C.M.A.'s plans. In 1972 the speaking tour idea sprung up again. Grange renewed his C.M.A. contacts and met in 1972 with C.M.A. officials in Montreal and British Columbia. Grange is known to be anxious to get into Quebec, which he considers a ripe market for his services. The industrialized west coast is another fertile area in his mind, Driver Pool sources claim.

The C.M.A. is acting out in its work with Grange a replay of the way national businessmen's lobbies in the United States helped strikebreaking spread in that country until the late 1930's. The C.M.A.'s American counterpart, the National Association of Manufacturers, did its part on behalf of the open shop.

The N.A.M., for example, circulated to all its members the notorious "Mohawk Valley Formula" for strikebreaking. The formula was a set of principles devised by James H. Rand Jr., former president of Remington Rand. He broke strikes in six Remington Rand plants in New York State's Mohawk River Valley following his principles. The "Mohawk Valley Formula", boiled down to its basics, was this:

1. When a strike is threatened, label the union leaders as "agitators," to discredit them with the public and their

own followers. . . . Disseminate propaganda falsely stating the issues involved in the strike so that the strikers appear to be making arbitrary demands, and the real issues, such as the employer's refusal to bargain collectively, are obscured. . . .

2. When the strike is called, raise high the banner of "law and order". . . .

3. Call a "mass meeting" of the citizens to co-ordinate public sentiment against the strike. . . .

4. Bring about the formation of a large armed police force to intimidate the strikers and to exert a psychological effect upon the citizens.

5. . . . Heighten the demoralizing effect of the above . . . by a "back-to-work" movement. . . .

6. . . . Even if the manoeuvre fails to induce a sufficient number of persons to return . . . persuade the public through pictures and news releases that the opening was nevertheless successful.

7. Stage the "opening" theatrically . . . having the employees march into the plant grounds in a massed group protected by squads of armed police. . . .

8. . . . If necessary, turn the locality into a warlike camp through the declaration of a state of emergency. . . .

9. Close the publicity barrage . . . on the theme that the plant is in full operation and that the strikers were merely a minority attempting to interfere with the "right to work . . ."[7]

The National Labour Relations Board ruled the "Mohawk Valley Formula" illegal.

In general, it is still a viable textbook for strikebreaking, which with few refinements is being used by Canadian employers who want to rid themselves of employees who need a union.

The National Association of Manufacturers' strikebreaking work was not unique. Another business group, the National Metal Trades Association, served 952 plants in the east and middle-west United States. No company that signed a union agreement could join that exclusive association. It passed out a black-list of union sympathizers to members. One of the senators on the La Follette committee that probed strikebreaking and wrote an eight-volume, 2,500,000-word report compared the National Trades Association with a union. A spokesman for the association was asked, "So you have an organization which has all the possibilities of collective action on the part of the employers?" The metal trades association man admitted management had formed something much like a union to beat the unions.[8]

A special "conference committee" of the National Association of Manufacturers also was discovered by the La Follette investigation. It included representatives of the country's 12 biggest corporations. The committee met in the executive suites of Standard Oil in New York City to discuss how to combat unions.[9]

If Grange and Canadian Driver Pool do manage to set up in Quebec, the likely front for the operation could be an inconspicuous cartage company on the Montreal waterfront called Vic's Cartage. Grange has visited the owner, Victor Barakett, several times in Montreal. Former associates remember that Barakett wined and dined Grange at the city's Playboy Club. Barakett visited Grange on occasion in Toronto. The two considered joining forces in a new cartage venture. Now, insiders believe Grange will try to use Vic's Cartage, with its warehouse and central location at 375 Ogilvy, as a base for a Quebec Driver Pool. Another location in Grange's expansion plans is Vancouver. Ex-partners say he plans to get a front to apply for a security-guard agency licence from the British Columbia government.

The Barakett friendship with Grange dates back several years, although friends find it hard to remember just how the connection developed. They say Barakett may have bought some cars from Grange when the strikebreaker was running C & C Sales in Toronto. Barakett sent Grange a Doberman pinscher puppy one Christmas.

Grange also dreams of expanding to the United States. He went to Chicago in 1972 to see executives of the American parents of one of his Ontario clients, says a source close to the organization.

If Grange and his imitators succeed in fanning out from Ontario across the country, the Ontario government will be one of those responsible, because they have not checked him in his home province. The province's news media will also be responsible. The newspapers of Toronto have obediently reported all the lies and half-truths Grange has told, about himself and about unions. They have failed to apply any scrutiny to the growing danger that strikebreaking presents to the public and to stable industrial relations in the province.

The fundamental reason why the media have gone soft on professional strikebreaking is that newspapers and much of the broadcasting industry outlets are themselves employers. They have a conflict of interest in anything they write or say about industrial relations. Their biggest sin is omission.

When Grange was convicted by a criminal court for wiretap conspiracy, not a single editorial was written by a newspaper in the province to condemn professional strikebreaking. The *Toronto Star* criticized the sentence, $500 fines for each defendant, as too lenient to deter wiretappers.

Although managements, newspaper editorial-writers and headline makers rant woefully that the cost of "inflationary" wage settlements must, inevitably, be borne by the consumer, one cannot find a newspaper, a politician in government or a business spokesman who has said that the extravagant fees handed over to professional strikebreakers must, inevitably, be passed on to the consumer. What part of the cost of Dare brand cookies will cover the money paid Canadian Driver Pool for its work during the 1972 strike by members of the Brewery Workers' Union in Kitchener, Ontario? What part of the gasoline price at Esso stations covers the strikebreaking fees paid Grange by Imperial Oil's subsidiary, Gilbarco Canada Limited in Brockville, Ontario?

The continent's press traditionally has been anti-labour (see Chapter 1). But the newspaper industry has managed to embellish strikebreaking with some tricks of its own that are unique in the world of big business.

The first "strike insurance" plans for employers were developed by newspaper publishers. The idea was copied by airlines and railroads in the United States.[10] The idea was born in the Newspaper Premium Fund Committee of the American Newspaper Publishers' Association, which has thoughtfully let Canadian publishers into the deal, too. The newspaper strike fund was first divulged in 1953, during a strike in Seattle, Washington. The publishers ran into problems in their own country, however, when state insurance authorities refused to approve the plan, labelling it contrary to public policy encouraging collective bargaining. It would be illegal for anyone to hold the premiums in the United States. So the publishers went to a more friendly country, where a friendly insurer offered to hang onto the publishers' premiums. The country was Canada, and the insurer was the Montreal Trust Company.[11]

Some known Canadian clients of the American strike insurance plan are prominent members of the Canadian Daily Newspaper Publishers' Association, the industry's lobby. The Vancouver *Sun* and the Vancouver *Province* are two subscribers, and they used the money during a lengthy strike and lockout in 1970. Another insured newspaper is the big Montreal daily, *La Presse*, according to spokesmen of the International Typographical Union. They say payments in the *La Presse* coverage include $10,000 a day for up to three months.

What newspaper strike-insurance and other employer mutual-defence pacts have done to collective bargaining in those industries is obvious. Newspapers have used the payments from their insurance to hire professional strikebreakers. And the newspaper industry's professional scabs are as violent a bunch as Canadian Driver Pool or the worst of the strikebreaking gangs for hire in the United States during the first half of the century from Pinkerton or the murderous crews of Pearl L. Bergoff.

"Police blotters . . .," says the I.T.U., "are soggy with the unlawful activities of strikebreakers" hired by newspaper publishers. The dossiers compiled by the I.T.U.-backed Presidents' Committee of Allied Printing and Related Trades would make a Dillinger cringe. Newspaper strikebreakers have been convicted of rape and attempted murder. Another was discharged from the military after a morals investigation that concerned a 10-year-old child. Another professional scab investigated by the printing trade unions is a convicted bank robber, and another was arrested for possession of a tear-gas gun. There are burglars, pornographic-literature peddlars, hit-and-run drivers, cheque forgers and bail jumpers in the files. All have been on newspaper payrolls during strikes.[12]

The publishers' santimonious editorials about law-and-order are morbidly laughable considering the calibre of employees the newspaper industry has used—and remunerated with huge salaries—to defeat unions.

The newspaper industry's long support of the professional strikebreaking racket has produced a few precedents. The first "school for scabs" was set up to help the publishing business defeat organized labour. One is the H. C. Haines Linotype School in Orlando, Florida.[13] I.T.U. spokesmen in Canada say publishers in this country prefer a "training school" that is also a non-union daily newspaper operation in Oklahoma. Newspapers in Toronto, Ottawa and other cities have sent supervisors to that state for training as strikebreakers..

The newspaper industry is probably the only business where scabs ever went on strike. It happened in 1957 during a strike by production workers for Griscom Publications, Incorporated, in Long Island, New York. The company published seven weekly newspapers. The strikebreakers were paid the standard scab rate in the news business, $300 to $400 a week (they worked a lot of overtime). After two weeks, however, Griscom balked at paying expenses for the strikebreakers, too, on top of such hefty weekly paycheques (this was 1957). The meal allowances and free hotel rooms were cut off, and the plant was shut by a strike of strikebreakers.[14]

The American newspaper industry had its own specialized service for professional strikebreakers, and the company doubtlessly funneled agents into Canada. It was run by a former lawyer with the grotesque name Bloor Schleppey. Like most strikebreaking moguls, he called himself a "counsel to management". His assistant was a former law student, Shirley Klein. An inquiry commission set up by the New York State government a few years ago reported that the Schleppey-Klein tandem had recruited "at least" 325 strikebreakers. More than 100 had worked two or more strikes. The American Newspaper Publishers' Association had Schleppey speak to publishers' gatherings but denied ever paying him.[15]

Schleppey claimed in 1958 that he had fought 30 strikes and lost "only a few". He took credit for heading off 70 other strikes by letting the employees know his linotype operators and other print-shop help were ready to come in.[16]

Publishers regularly screech during negotiations that union proposals, especially in the production end of the business are "featherbedding". But the press barons see no contradiction in hiring "stand-bys" at full pay and with all expenses taken care of, waiting for a strike.

The growth of newspaper chains has let publishers transfer help from one branch of the corporation to another to break strikes. But the publishers also co-operate with each other, defying the first principle of business, competition, that they piously preach in their editorial, news and advertising columns. John Bassett, publisher of the now-defunct *Toronto Telegram,* dispatched scabs from his own non-union production room to *The Ottawa Citizen* during a strike and lockout of composing room employees in 1970. So did *The Globe and Mail.*

Even purportedly fierce cross-town rivals like *The Ottawa Citizen* and *The Ottawa Journal* drop their role as combatants when it's time to fight the unions. In 1972, the I.T.U. complained to the Ontario Labour Relations Board that the *Journal* had refused to sign a negotiated contract until its rival, the *Citizen,* had concluded a settlement with the Typographical Union. After the folding of *The Telegram* was announced in September, 1971, publisher Bassett sabotaged a committee that was trying to find work for his 1,200 employees when federal Manpower Department officials refused to let him use the committee to send scabs to strike-bound *La Presse* in Quebec. Bassett had wanted the Manpower Department to pay the travel costs of sending the strikebreakers to help the French-language paper, which is a part of the mammoth Power Corporation conglomerate.

The smashing of the I.T.U. in the composing rooms of the three Toronto papers in 1964 (with nearly 900 replacements) changed dramatically the image and voice of organized labour in Canada, say veteran labour-beat reporters and union leaders.

The amount of labour news declined sharply in the Toronto newspapers. The Toronto papers combine as a powerful influence on what the rest of Canada reads in its local papers and sees and hears on its national television and radio news programmes. The Toronto labour-news blackout has made a perceptible if not measurable impact. Liberal party Senator Keith Davey pointed it out in a 1969 speech to the Senate, when he proposed his special committee on the mass media. The strike officially had not been called off, and it wasn't ended until late 1971. "One cannot help wondering," Davey said, "how many editorials would have appeared in the Toronto press had any other Toronto industry been similarly strikebound for such a long period of time. . . ."[17]

In light of the anti-labour news and employment practices of the nation's press, it was ironic that the defence in the Grange and Barry Chapman conspiracy trial would claim that the wiretap found by the Redpath Sugar strikers actually may have been planted by the strikers themselves. Lawyer David Humphrey, representing police constable Chapman, commented to one union witness, "This wiretap being found was such a good thing, I suppose you wondered why you didn't think of it yourself."[18] When Humphrey suggested to Ralph Forsey, president of the striking local, that finding the tape recorder "was great", Forsey replied, "Well it wouldn't help us with the company, no."

HUMPHREY: It would be great in propaganda point of view.

FORSEY: We weren't interested in propaganda. We were interested in a better contract.[19]

Canadian Driver Pool and Richard Grange generally have received a favourable press. Grange's biggest "play" was a front-page feature story in the *Toronto Star* on Saturday, November 20, 1971. The story's headline proclaimed that "At 27, he makes $250,000 a year." A picture accompanying the story, by free-lance photographer Horst Ehricht, portrayed Grange with a Doberman pinscher. The strikebreaker posed with his right arm tucked inside his sport coat, Napoleon fashion. So good-looking and prosperous was the man in the picture, that at least one *Star* reader, Irving Geller, wrote Grange begging for a job. He was hired.

The weekly newspaper where Grange lived wrote him up, too. (Grange lived in suburban Toronto in a penthouse at 7 Roanoke Road in Don Mills at the time, but in 1972 he moved to a $65,000 home at 95 Francine Drive farther north in the Toronto borough of North York.)

This paper reported that the North York resident had been threatened with death after the big splash in the *Star*. The story also carried, without apparently checking with the police, Grange's claim that a bullet had been fired "through his car".[20] The weekly is owned by the *Toronto Star*.

A *Star* story on May 15, 1972, about the lengthy Steelworkers' strike at Gidon Industries in northwestern Metropolitan Toronto, was headlined, 'Canada's biggest union fights the 'strike preventers' ". It quoted Grange: "I wouldn't say we are strikebreakers. We are more along the line of strike pre-venters."

It repeated Grange's boasts that Driver Pool uses "aircraft patrols" and "infra-red cameras which take pictures at night". (There have been no aircraft patrols. And there is no such thing as an "infra-red camera". There is infra-red film, which can be used in a camera to take nighttime pictures, but sources near the Driver Pool camp doubt that Grange's cameramen bother with it.)

The headline "biggest union" also helped perpetrate the myth of union power that the press has created over the years. This has been done while subtly downplaying the truth about professional strikebreaking. An early *Star* story on Grange's arrest in the Redpath wiretap investigation was head-lined: "Constable arrested with businessman in wiretap case".[21]

The list of unions smashed in Ontario—50 since 1965—repudiates the myth of labour power. So does a comparison of assets between unions and the corporations they bargain with. The total assets of the 11 biggest unions in Canada are less than the assets of the Steel Company of Canada Limited, or the assets of Ford Motor Company of Canada or MacMillan Bloedel

Limited. The assets of all the unions in the country and the parent unions of international labour organizations operating in Canada are less than the assets of International Nickel and only slightly larger than the assets of Imperial Oil. The assets banked in Canada of all the unions operating in the country are less than the assets of any one of the companies in this list: Moore Corporation, Thomson Newspapers, Cominco, Goodyear Tire and Rubber of Canada, Dominion Stores, Canadian Breweries, Hudson's Bay Mining and Smelting.[22]

For the country's biggest newspaper, the *Toronto Star,* slanting the news about strikebreaking isn't enough. In April, 1972, the *Star* gave Grange real journalism status—and made him a sacred cow. One of the paper's top investigative reporters and a photographer pieced together a damaging story on Driver Pool and its front company, Canadian Specialized Security Limited. The story plainly indicated that Driver Pool employees were guarding a struck plant. It told how the reporter had approached two strikeguards at Macotta Company of Canada Limited and that these men had failed to produce security-guard licences when asked, as licenced guards are required to do by law. The story also pointed out that a $2,000 fine could be levied for failure to show a guard's licence.

The story was never printed. *Star* sources say publisher Beland H. Honderich personally killed the story, although the newspaper's lawyers had checked it and cleared it for libel. Honderich gave as his reason for killing the piece that the exposé didn't show a real threat to the public, a criterion that Honderich presumably holds up to all stories in his paper. James Tannian, Richard's Grange's publicist, takes credit for squelching the story, according to a Driver Pool source. But there are obviously other reasons why the newspaper publisher would not want to raise public outrage in his news columns about a strikebreaking agency operating illegally. One of Grange's best customers for his truck-rental business was the *Toronto Star.*

Notes

1. C.M.A. membership bulletin, March 24, 1966.
2. Convention programme, 100th Annual General Meeting, June 6, 7, 8, 1971, Royal York Hotel, p. 13.
3. *The Globe and Mail,* April 18, 1970.
4. *The Globe and Mail,* April 13, 1966.
5. *The Globe and Mail,* June 14, 1966.

6. Lipton, Charles, *The Trade Union Movement of Canada 1827-1959*, Canadian Social Publications Limited, Montreal, 1966, p. 112.
7. Taylor and Witney, *op. cit.,* pp. 125, 540-542.
8. Amidon, *op. cit.,* pp. 305-306.
9. Ward, Paul W., "Washington Week," *The Nation,* February 27, 1937, p. 231.
10. *Labour Relations and the Law in the United Kingdom and the United States,* Michigan International Labour Studies, Volume 1, University of Michigan, Ann Arbor, Michigan, 1968, p. 197.
11. Barry, John, "Strike Insurance: A Threat to Collective Bargaining," *The American Federationist,* publication of the A.F.L.-C.I.O., March, 1961.
12. Presidents' Committee of Allied Printing and Related Trades, Legislative Subcommittee, *Spotlight on the Third Pollution,* Colorado Springs, Colorado, 1969.
13. Catherwood report, *op. cit.,* p. 15.
14. *Ibid.,* pp. 18-19.
15. *Ibid.,* pp. 7-8.
16. "The Strikebreaker," *Time,* April 28, 1958, pp. 66, 69.
17. Speech in the Senate, February 4, 1969.
18. Trial transcript, *op. cit.,* p. 178.
19. *Ibid.,* p. 177.
20. *The North York Mirror/Enterprise,* November 24, 1971, p. 1.
21. *Toronto Star,* October 16, 1971, p. 1.
22. "Another slant on myth that unions have too much power," *The Provincial,* publication of the British Columbia Government Employees' Union, February, 1972, p. 3.

7

The Spies Among Us

"I feel a man running a business must keep himself posted on how that business is being run."

> *Robert Pinkerton II, grandson of the founder, Pinkerton's Detective Agency, testifying before the U.S. Senate committee investigation of anti-labour espionage*[1]

The assaults by hired toughs, the lamed pickets hit by scab trucks and the surveillance by mercenary strikeguards are the overt faces of professional strikebreaking. There is a darkened, concealed side to professional unionbusting in Canada that almost no one acknowledges. It is anti-union espionage.

Some spies are recruited by detective agencies; more are enlisted by so-called "management" consultants". Anti-labour spying is conducted by two means: with paid operatives sent among the workers to spy on union sympathizers and sabotage their organizing efforts by disclosing the leaders to management; and with employees themselves who are "hooked" cloak-and-dagger fashion by professional unionbusters, who pay their worker-agents for regular reports on the daily behaviour of their fellow employees.

The number of labour spies in Canadian industry is incalculable. It can probably be said that they exist in every industry. The U.S. Senate Committee on Education and Labour that reported on industrial espionage and other violations of the civil rights of union sympathizers said:

> From motion-picture producers to steel makers, from hookless fasteners to automobiles, from small units to giant enterprises—scarcely an industry . . . is not fully represented in the list of clients of the detective agencies. Large corporations rely on spies. No firm is too small to employ them.[2]

Rulings of the National Labour Relations Board administering The National Labour Relations Act (or the Wagner Act, as it also was known) made anti-union espionage illegal in the United States even before the Second World War.

The practice appears to have ebbed gradually in the U.S., and its perpetrators have confessed and publicly atoned. Robert Pinkerton said when it was over that the infiltration of unions "is a phase of our business that we are not particularly proud of and we're delighted we're out of it".[3]

Even the capitalists who bankrolled the labour-spy system renounced it after Senator Robert La Follette Jr.'s probe had exposed the racket. The labour-relations director for General Motors, Harry W. Anderson, said he had personally opposed labour espionage "for a long time . . . this investigation gave us the opportunity to wipe it out". In 1935 and 1936 G.M. paid detective agencies almost $1 million for anti-union spying.[4] An economist with the National Labour Relations Board told the La Follette hearing that there was a "spy in every local". If there were 40,000 spies (one of the lower estimates given the committee by spy-rackets witnesses), then at contemporary rates it was costing $80 million a year for American industry to peep into the private thoughts of its employees.[5]

The La Follette committee's disclosures ripped away the camouflage of industrial espionage. Witnesses told how "hooked" employees were indoctrinated by the spy agencies, assigned code numbers and directed to mail their daily reports to post-office boxes. Some workers were dupes and didn't even know that their reports were spy papers used in defeating unions. One master spy, C. M. "Red" Kuhl, told the committee how new agents are recruited:

> Well, first you look your prospect over, and if he is married that is preferable. If he is financially hard up, that is number two. If his wife wants more money or hasn't got a car, that all counts. And you go offer him this extra money. *Naturally you don't tell him what you want him for.* You have got some story that you are representing some bankers or some bondholders or an insurance company and they want to know what goes on in there. (*Emphasis added.*)[6]

The potential spy's name comes from the company that wants the information about its workers. Occasionally, a worker-spy discerned what he was being used for and despaired, like the spy who wrote to Railway Audit and Inspection Company, a spy agency:

I may as well state that Ferguson . . . and Kepler [both union men] are personal friends of mine. I have known Ferguson for 20 years and Kepler for 10 years, and now I am selling them out, as they tell me most anything.[7]

For selling out their colleagues, as this spy put it, anti-union espionage agents were paid $25 to $75 a month (this was in the late 1930's). In Canada today the going rate is higher, but not much; allowing for inflation, spies in this country go much cheaper.

Before laws were passed in the United States (and later in Canada) to make it illegal to dismiss union sympathizers, "ring leaders" exposed by the industrial spy were usually fired.*
Later managements got a little softer and used the spy's reports to set up and control company unions.

The disclosures from the La Follette probe could have provided the textbooks for industrial-spy outfits operating in Ontario and other parts of Canada today. Maybe they were. There is a feeling, however, that "it can't happen here". But it does. Even the historian of the federal government's $2-million Task Force on Labour Relations said "the use of professional labour spies and strikebreakers" in Canada has been "relatively rare". But he hedged a bit and added that "this is difficult to prove conclusively".[8]

The impact is probably the same even if Canadian historians have refused to look for the spies in their midst. Anti-labour espionage has been devastating on the growth of organized labour. "The evidence is overwhelming," said the U.S. strike-breaking and espionage investigation, "that the use of this labour espionage is demonstrated and proved to be one of the

---

*Although provincial labour laws purport to outlaw dismissals and other reprisals for organizing unions, firings are regular occurrences in organizing campaigns. Researchers for the Ontario Department of Labour reported in 1966 that a study of more than 700 unfair labour-practice complaints in a five-year period revealed that 85 to 90 per cent allege employees were discharged for union activity. There is little followup on what happens to those lucky enough to be reinstated by the Labour Relations Board. But a U.S. study indicates that the worker dismissed for union activity, possibly on the report of a labour spy, is effectively blacklisted—at least where he or she had tried to form a union. Less than half the dismissed workers ever do return to their jobs, according to the U.S. figures, which were derived from National Labour Relations Board cases from 1962 to 1964. Three-quarters of the reinstated union activists were gone from the company within two years. Most gave company retaliation as the reason for leaving.

most effective weapons in destroying genuine labour collective bargaining activities on the part of workers."[9]

The most successful labour spies posed as union supporters. Some rose to astonishing positions in the labour organizations they were subverting. One was the president of a local labour council. Another exposed by the La Follette committee was president of the Georgia state federation of labour. He was even nominated for president. Pinkerton's claimed 100 union officials on its spy payroll, including the national vice-president of one labour organization.[10]

The source of industrial espionage is the same anti-union climate that permits the more overt forms of unionbusting and strikebreaking. Corporate oligarchs believe it is their right to know everything about their employees, just as they believe it is their right to break up their workers' organizations. A loosely-enforced law like the Labour Relations Act with its purported prohibition on "interference" in trade unions is hardly a challenge to a union-hating capitalist.

Management spy agencies run their networks like military intelligence systems. The analogy is appropriate because those spied on for the real military and the captains of industry are both perceived as enemies. The government of Ontario tolerates anti-union espionage and has made the province an especially fertile area for spying. The government has even had its own spy system to gather secret intelligence against its political enemies: "the Ontario Gestapo" of ex-Premier George Drew, a political foe called it. The government's own spy agency was exposed in 1945 during the provincial election campaign by Edward B. Jolliffe, leader of the Co-operative Commonwealth Federation (C.C.F.). Jolliffe contended that Drew had maintained his secret police as a special branch of the Ontario Provincial Police. The reports of the branch—financed by public money, but revenue unauthorized by the legislature—were fed to government officials and Conservative party propagandists. "Spies were sent to union meetings," Jolliffe said in a province-wide radio broadcast. "Blacklists of people of whom the Gestapo disapproved were prepared, and big business was given the opportunity of checking their [employees] against them." Reports were compiled by O.P.P. Captain William J. Osborne-Dempster. He signed them with the code number "D-208".[11]

(The allegations didn't help Jolliffe's party. The Drew government set up a royal commission to investigate Jolliffe's accusations but refused the demand of the opposition parties that the election be postponed until the commission reported its findings. The C.C.F., the official opposition before the 1945 election, fell to eight seats, and Drew's minority government gained majority status. The royal commission proved "the basic substance" of Jolliffe's charges "beyond the shadow of a doubt", according to historians. Strangely, nowhere in the government can a complete copy of the royal commission's proceedings be found.)[12]

Union officers have been aggressively sought out as company spies, and rank-and-file spies are encouraged to take part in the union and try to take it over. One spy discovered in the International Union of Mine, Mill and Smelterworkers' Union at Sudbury (where the union represents Falconbridge Nickel Mines Limited miners) was a steward. Another in the same union was on the local's executive board. Mining town spies for management were exposed as early as the 1930's, and oldtime mine organizers believe spies were commonplace in northern Ontario.

The R.C.M.P. has kept close tabs on the union movement, especially in industries like mining and other resource-based industries that governments consider critical. Spies often are thought at once to be R.C.M.P. plants, but most probably work for private spy rings. One spy uncovered in Sudbury in the early 1950's was thought to be an R.C.M.P. man (old union leaders say they gave him 24 hours to leave town, and he did). Actually the man later admitted working for a spy company in Toronto called Wiliam R. Brock and Associates Limited. The Brock firm still exists.

The R.C.M.P. still keeps up contacts with union members in at least one industry, oil refining.

Art Stone, a worker at the British American Oil Limited refinery (now Gulf Oil Canada Limited) in Clarkson, Ontario, west of Toronto, says the R.C.M.P. first contacted him in 1965. He was asked what he knew about several members of his union, the Oil, Chemical and Atomic Workers' International Union. The Mounties, says Stone, had heard a tape recording purportedly of remarks made by an O.C.A.W. local president. Stone learned later the tape had been edited to make the other unionist sound like an extremist. "The R.C.M.P. got my name from somebody in the B. A. office," says Stone. "I never found out who the hell gave them my name."

For the R.C.M.P., union espionage is the secret side of its anti-labour work. Historian Stuart Jamieson says the role of the country's national police in labour-management disputes on the side of corporate power "in all probability has had a profound effect on the climate of labour relations in this country".[13] (See Chapter 1.) The R.C.M.P. has contacts in other parts of the country in the oil refineries, say O.C.A.W. officials. While the R.C.M.P. kept its eye on mine-workers' organizers, it didn't —or wouldn't—care about the mine owners and their agents. On February 24, 1942, a gang of International Nickel Company supervisors broke into the Mine-Mill union office in Sudbury, wrecked it and savagely beat two union members.

(The R.C.M.P.'s wide-ranging interest in the lives of the country's citizens doesn't stop at unions, long a target of hunts for "subversive" elements. A new interest is the campus. Government officials willingly co-operate. The Ontario Department of Education says some school principals have been providing R.C.M.P. officers with student records for some time. An R.C.M.P. spokesman assures everyone "there is nothing ulterior going on". He calls the investigations "security checks".[14]

There is evidence that industrial espionage in Ontario is going on in the mining and oil-refining industries and also in trucking, baking, foods and all types of manufacturing enterprises. Unions that have been infiltrated by industrial spies include the International Brotherhood of Teamsters, the Oil, Chemical and Atomic Workers' International Union, the International Chemical Workers' Union, Mine-Mill, and the United Steelworkers of America. That is doubtlessly a short list.

There are two principal camouflages that spies use to infiltrate and work against unions. The first is witch-hunting. Spies are told that they are helping to purge radicals and subversives from industry. The second is security. Employers say that secret agents among their workers are hired to catch pilfering employees.

The La Follette committee that probed anti-union espionage and strikebreaking in the U.S. found that security was the excuse used most frequently by the detective agencies supplying anti-labour spies.

The security stories "were of so little merit that after examination by the Committee they were repudiated by the same officials who advanced them", La Follette reported.[15] The "subversives" line also turned out to be a subterfuge when put under scrutiny by the committee. One journalist following La Follette's disclosures reported: "The detective agencies who employ these labour spies habitually raise a 'Red scare', seeking to identify all labour with extreme radicalism. They admitted on the witness stand that there is hardly ever any truth in these charges, but explained coolly that they helped to make public opinion anti-union."[16]

"Red scare" has been the technique favoured by one of the most experienced labour-spy agencies in Ontario, William B. McDougall Associates Limited. One document sent a McDougall operative in the trucking industry was the monthly *News Letter* of the Canadian Chamber of Commerce for October, 1961. Here are excerpts from the *News Letter*:

The threat of Communism is today closer to Canada and to Canadians than at any time in the past.

. . . . .

Look for their support of everything which helps to concentrate power in the hands of the Government, thereby depriving the individual of that power. The breakdown of personal freedom which leads to a greater acceptance of Government action curtailing that freedom, paves the way for the gradual acceptance of communism.

. . . . .

The threat is real and the danger is imminent. The Communists are predicting that communism will rule the world in 10 to 15 years. If we don't take steps to protect our freedom today, tomorrow may be too late.

. . . . .

The easy acceptance of socialistic doctrine without thoughtful consideration of where it may lead is today's greatest threat to individual freedom.

McDougall's operatives also received editions of a right-wing publication called *Clip-Sheet,* published in Toronto. Typical issues of *Clip-Sheet* warn "vastly enlarged state spending . . . has curtailed private investment and limited economic growth" (December 12, 1962). Another cautions, "Organized labour cannot evade its share of the responsibility for promoting economic expansion. Its concern cannot be limited solely to benefits for union members" (September 26, 1962).

Newspaper articles discrediting the labour movement were sent regularly to McDougall spies—in plain envelopes with no return address.

Contact with McDougall's potential labour spies was made through names supplied by the company. Contact often started with a telephone call, like the one that William Lavender of McDougall Associates made to a Hamilton, Ontario, truck driver. Lavender, a tall man with gray hair, somewhat distinguished-looking, came to the trucker's house one Sunday afternoon. The driver was asked to mail daily reports on what he observed around his company, Hanson Transport (now called Canadian Freightways). "He [Lavender] said it would be beneficial to the employees I was working with," recalls the trucker, a member of the International Brotherhood of Teamsters. "He asked if I had any complaints at work." The Teamster told him one or two. "He said, 'We can get to the companies, you don't have to go through the union for better working conditions.'" Lavender asked him to write down the grievances of the other employees in the company, and he asked, were the employees dissatisfied with the union?

"He said, 'We're just working for the trucking industry and we have a group of companies working this way,'" the Teamster recalls.

For his reports the trucker received $80 a month, deposited in a numbered bank account at the Bank of Nova Scotia in downtown Toronto. He made withdrawals at the bank's branch in Stoney Creek, where he lived just north of Hamilton. He was assigned a code number. "We never use names," he says Lavender told him.

Later Lavender met the Teamster at McDougall's office, at the time at 5317A Yonge Street in the northern part of Metropolitan Toronto. (The agency moved later to 5543 Yonge Street. In 1972 McDougall moved out of town to Bethany, Ontario, northwest of Peterborough, and closed his Toronto office.)

At the offices, a small suite above a row of stores, the Teamster was told the agency was not satisfied with his reports. They wanted more information for their clients. Lavender walked him across the street for lunch. Lavender then told him "other people in Hamilton are dissatisfied" and want to get out of the union. After this meeting, the Teamster went to union officials, who asked him to play along with Lavender and try to get more information. He sent in some phoney reports, and his payments soon stopped.

Another Teamster in Toronto met William B. McDougall, who dropped by twice at the union member's home (unannounced) to ask him to spy. The man says McDougall said the Teamster was picked because he was one of a few men who had worked several years for his employer, the Canada Bread Division of American-owned Corporate Foods Limited. He was assigned a number, F18, and told to send his reports to a post-office box that McDougall Associates had rented, Box 206, in care of the post office at Willowdale, a north-suburban area of Metropolitan Toronto. McDougall told him he would pay the Teamster $80 a month for weekly reports on what he observed about Canada Bread's employees. The new recruit says that no mention was made of the union he was to spy on, Local 647 of the International Brotherhood of Teamsters. But later the recruit was asked to come to McDougall's office, where he was directed to supply more specific details in his communications on the union members and their meetings.

McDougall himself, the agency's founder, apparently got his training and developed his methods at another busy spy enterprise, William R. Brock and Associates. McDougall worked with Brock almost from the beginning at its 24 King Street West office, rose to "sales manager" in 1956 and to vice-president in 1960. Another graduate of Brock was William Lavender, who later worked with McDougall. The Brock office today is at 100 Adelaide Street West, Suite 1505, in downtown Toronto. Brock and Associates were set up in 1947. The original directors, with Brock himself, his wife, Mary, and son Marshall, were lawyers, who apparently found the firm's services valuable and would recommend Brock to their management clients.

The first lawyer in the company, Edward Neil Johnson, quit as director in 1954 and was replaced by J. T. Garrow. Robert W. Davies, a partner in Garrow's law office, was added in 1956. In 1958 new leaders came to Brock's. One of the most important additions to the company was Edward A. Sinkewicz, who became a vice-president and is considered the driving force behind the company today. The company's legal business changed firms, and the new firm was Mathews, Dinsdale and Clark, one of the busiest management legal offices in southern Ontario. The firm has many lawyers, and most of them act as labour-relations advisers to a variety of companies in construction and manufacturing, often handling negotiations.

The president of Brock and Associates today is Joseph Daniel Arcouiet, who changed the euphemism for the company's real business to "personnel" from "industrial engineers" (the original Brock's name for this work).

The company has received hundreds of reports a week from

its worker-spies in the plants and offices of its clients and summarized them for management eyes, according to a former employee.

Labour-spy reports often sound innocuous. One report from a spy at Falconbridge Nickel Mines Limited in Sudbury related a membership meeting of the Mine, Mill and Smelterworkers' Union. Dutifully following instructions to capitalize all names, the spy described alleged talk of a strike:

> "One of GILLIS' strong supporters, I think I can get his name later, followed STEWART and said that if at the next membership meeting there was a large turn out he himself would move a motion for these days of mourning. He stated that it was by this means that John L [sic] Lewis was able to win most of his concessions from the mine owners.
>
> "It was a great night for GILLIS. His supporters were in the majority by at least 20 to 1."

This operative, Code number C 143, mailed his reports to "W. L. Hogan, P.O. Box 503, Toronto, Ontario". "W. L. Hogan" appears to be a phoney name. The spy apparently was recruited by William R. Brock and Associates of Toronto, which had contacted Falconbridge employees.

In 1960 McDougall left Brock and Associates to set up his own industrial-espionage agency. McDougall took some of Brock's clients with him. One big client, International Nickel Company of Canada Limited, still buys the services of Brock and Associates. McDougall's firm, like Brock's, was deeply involved with members of the law profession. He called himself "personnel consultant". The objects of the new concern, according to the charter issued for the company by the Ontario government, are:

> To act as counsellors, consultants and advisers in general to management executives, members and associates of any institution, association, commercial enterprise or industrial organization.

Nothing in the stated purposes of the company indicated that the means to be used to act as "consultants and advisers" to management would be a network of spies. Nothing said that literally crates of files would be needed to keep the reports of the many operatives that McDougall intended to sign up, and nothing was said of what future use these files would be when the client was finished with the spy.

It is strange that the industrial espionage business, whose propaganda so vigorously despises socialism and so fanatically opposes "radicalism" and links it to communism, should use in its everyday business a system of spying that might rival Hitler's S.S. or Stalin's secret police, in the number of its operatives and extent of its organization. It is obvious that the most ardent apostles of "freedom" work through the totalitarian tactic of furtive spying, certainly an antithesis of anyone's conception of freedom and democracy. Three prominent Toronto lawyers, one later to be a vice-president of the Canadian Bar Association and a member of the Ontario Labour Relations Board, incorporated McDougall's company. The lawyers were Walter Gibson Cassels, John Frederick Mitchell and George S. P. Ferguson, all partners in 1961 when William B. McDougall organized the firm with the lawyers. Ferguson, the Canadian Bar Association vice-president, was to serve as a management appointee to the Labour Relations Board, which is supposed to foster collective bargaining between unions and employers and protect the right of workers to organize without interference to improve their working conditions and standard of living.

Ferguson has been the architect of some crucial labour struggles since he helped put the McDougall spy agency in business, notably the 1969 Hanes Hosiery strike in Toronto, where the strikers' union was smashed (see Chapter 3).

McDougall's propagandizing and the prosyletizing of other spy-ring leaders against "communism" is a familiar deception in anti-labour espionage. It is a favourite banner carried by most counterfeit champions of liberty who are themselves autocrats. The "special branch" of the O.P.P. set up by former Premier Drew nominally was looking for communists and other enemies of the state. But, says a historian, its primary interest was to combat "not communism, but the C.C.F. party".[17]

McDougall's major manual for worker-operatives dispels his staunch defence of "freedom" and exposes the labour-spy racket as a refuge for manipulators who don't hesitate to use bribery to destroy working-class organizations. These organizations supposedly are protected by the labour laws and the freedom of association passage of the Bill of Rights.

McDougall calls his tactics "man engineering". The phrase was lifted from the American spy agencies, which often called their management services "human engineering".[18] What is McDougall's "human engineering"? The manual doesn't define it precisely, but what emerges from his brainwashing of the worker is the notion that management's goals are the workers' goals, that management's motives are good motives. His own work McDougall cloaks in piety. "It would require volumes to thoroughly explain each separate phase of the magnitude and scope of our work, the great good which is being accomplished and the far-reaching effects on industry in general," begins a typical indoctrination of a labour spy. Wary new recruits are reassured that their stealthy job is honest, even noble: "You are performing an act worthy of highest distinction."

"Our work is interesting and is the greatest teacher of human nature," McDougall expounds in another section. "It is most honourable, humanitarian and very important, and must be recognized as such."

The therapeutic treatment having ended, the manual begins its instructions. "The average employee," it says, regards himself as ignored and neglected by his employer, simply because he does not understand his employer's motives." The goal of "human engineering" is "to change negative ideas to constructive motives . . . ." The result is "our constructive influence on the large body of workers with resultant improvement in their welfare, happiness and contentment".

Then comes instruction on the methods: "Become a leader among the workers in all forms of activity. . . and gradually bring about a complete understanding between the workers and the management . . . which will eventually result in as near a cooperative, loyal and efficient force of workers and plant operation as possible."

Finally, details to remember: "Adhere strictly to the procedure required," commands the spy book. In his or her reports, the operative is ordered to "be sure to show what makes the workers feel the way they do". The operative is to pick out "conservative", "neutral" and "negative" employees. The "conservative" worker is the best. The "conservative" worker works hard, doesn't complain, likes the boss.

The spies are told to attend meetings (such as union meetings) and write down what everyone says, "word by word as near as they can be remembered". Even if the meeting is on the spy's day off, the spy must attend. Don't use the same mailbox every night. It would catch someone's attention. If the spy meets another "contact" in the same shop or office, ignore him. Reverse all charges on telephone calls (but don't use switchboards).

The result of the spy's work, the manual promises, will be a "constructive mental attitude" by the workers spied upon and "conservatism towards employer and government". A "destructive mental attitude would result in "low production", "waste", "absenteeism" and "strikes".

How many men and women do this "honourable, humanitarian and very important" work is impossible to say. At the zenith of the spy-racket business in the United States, it was said that there was a spy in every union local, or perhaps 41,000 spies.[19] There are 9,593 locals in Canada.[20]

Into the spy organization that McDougall was building in 1965 came one of the most mysterious figures in Canadian labour-management relations, Hugh Brian Gallagher. He is one of the most successful industrial spies in the country, mercenary enough to work for both management and, on at least one occasion, a union bureaucrat. Brian Gallagher was born in 1932. He had the prospects of an exceptional policeman and undercover agent. He joined the R.C.M.P. when he was only 19. According to R.C.M.P. records he resigned in 1958 and dropped out of sight. The R.C.M.P. claims Gallagher rejoined in September, 1960. Much of his time was spent apparently tailing union activists. He apparently was loaned by the R.C.M.P. for a time to Upper Lakes Shipping Limited during the recognition strikes and disturbances that entangled the Seafarers' International Union. A former S.I.U. member believes Gallagher was a bodyguard for John D. Leitch, president of Upper Lakes. At this time it is believed Gallagher met Bernard Merrigan, the former security-agency figure who became an executive of Upper Lakes (see Chapter 5). Gallagher resigned from the R.C.M.P. again in May 1965 and almost immediately went to work for William B. McDougall Associates Limited. It is important that the R.C.M.P. claims Gallagher resigned. Many people in the union movement treat Gallagher as if he is still an R.C.M.P. agent. They believe that if he isn't actually an agent, he has a special relationship with the R.C.M.P. The R.C.M.P deny it—vigorously. McDougall, the spy-agency president, says Gallagher did "recruiting" for him. McDougall says he hired Gallagher because the former R.C.M.P. officer had vast contacts. Gallagher's occupation was listed at the time as "salesman". Whatever he really did for McDougall, Gallagher didn't do it for long. He resigned in October, 1965, says McDougall. Since then Gallagher has not had a detectable full-time job.

Shortly after Gallagher quit the Mounties, according to one source in the R.C.M.P., and while he was working for McDougall, he came to Sgt. Bruce Ruddick of the R.C.M.P. with an important "tip". He reported that he had become aware of a plot to set off an explosion in the Clarkson, Ontario refinery of the British American Oil Company. The R.C.M.P. investigated but could not substantiate Gallagher's story. What is curious is that at the same time John Kane, an officer of the Oil, Chemical and Atomic Workers local at the refinery, was approached by one of the supervisors, who offered a deal. The supervisor, says Kane, said he wanted to help the union, which was on strike against the company. If Kane would get the dynamite, Kane says the supervisor told him, the supervisor would blow up a water-pump operation in the refinery. Kane told him no, emphatically. Until 1972, says Kane, he never discussed the proposed bomb with the R.C.M.P. or anyone else. The way Gallagher learned how to tip off Sgt. Ruddick of the Mounties about the "plot" remains a mystery.

The trail of Brian Gallagher is littered with such intrigue. For a time he worked for Russell M. Tolley & Associates Limited, a company that manages welfare and pension funds for many unions. Gallagher's association with Tolley's would put him in touch with lengthy lists of members of several unions, lists that would be valuable for spy work.

Richard Dobie, the manager of Tolley's headquarters in Toronto, trusted Gallagher enough to give him a company credit card and a key to the office. He gave him a company car to use. He claims, however, that Gallagher never actually worked full-time for Tolley. Dobie says Gallagher handled calls for welfare-plan payments and other problems that cropped up at night. "He pops up everywhere," Dobie says. Many people who once knew Gallagher flinch when asked about their association with him. Dobie claims he has nothing more to do with him. So does another long-time friend, Bernard Merrigan, the shipping company negotiator and former private investigator and security-guard boss in Quebec.

In Port Credit, Ontario, Gallagher "popped up" in an investigation of electronic eavesdropping equipment discovered in the office next to the Oil, Chemical and Atomic Workers' International Union headquarters in 1965 during the B.A. strike. A microphone had been imbedded in the concrete wall of the adjoining offices. There was proof that a telephone had been tapped. Port Credit police detectives removed the equipment but say today that they don't know what happened to the devices they seized.

Finding the "bugs" during the O.C.A.W.'s strike wasn't the only suspicious occurrence during the strike at B.A. (Gulf Oil today). Two ex-convicts posing as private investigators tried to sell the union what they said were tape recordings made by the hidden "bugs" for $5,000. J. Ronald Duncan, the Union's Canadian director at the time, didn't take the offer. The men were identified from photographs and licence plates as Edwin (Eddie) McDonald and Bill Sims, both friends of Brian Gallagher. Sims subsequently admitted to a private investigator that he, McDonald and Gallagher all were involved in the electronic eavesdropping on the O.C.A.W. offices.

In practically every bargaining situation or major organizing drive at Gulf Oil since then, Brian Gallagher has "popped up". Richard Dobie claims that he saw Gallagher entering Gulf's offices several times. He also says that Gallagher worked for a time in Gulf's credit department, but the oil company claims Gallagher's name does not show on the payroll lists in its personnel department. Although Gallagher told him after he left McDougall Associates in 1965 that he was a private investigator, Dobie says, there is no record that he has ever held an investigator's licence in Ontario.

Gallagher also is believed to have been in Kingston, Ontario, during a strike by the International Union of District 50 in 1965. A District 50 official says he identified Gallagher from photographs as being at the picket lines when disturbances erupted sparked by rumours that Du Pont intended to ship goods from the strikebound plant. There were no shipments.

In 1967 Gallagher became for a brief time a staff representative of the International Brotherhood of Teamsters in Toronto. He was placed on the personal staff of the union's Canadian director at the time, I. M. (Casey) Dodds. His job appears to have been to help Dodds crush dissidents and opponents in the Teamsters' southern Ontario operations. Gallagher at this time was introducing his friend Eddie McDonald as another representative of the Teamsters. At the Park Plaza Hotel one day, three rooms side by side were taken for a special meeting. In one of the rooms, say Teamster union sources, was Brian Gallagher. In another was Eddie McDonald. A trap to frame the dissident unionists was set in motion with an offer to them that Casey Dodds would be killed if the dissidents came up with $25,000. They didn't take the offer.

In the same year, right-wing-inspired hate mail poured out to members of the province-wide Teamster Local 938 attacking the dissident officials. The nature of the propaganda mailed is generally described as "red-baiting". An investigation traced the postage metre on the envelopes. The hate mail to slander the dissidents had been postmarked in the offices of Russell

M. Tolley & Associates, at the time when Brian Gallagher had free access to the premises.

In 1970 Gallagher showed up again, O.C.A.W. officials believe. The union began negotiating in Nova Scotia at the new facility of Canadian General Electric, at Port Hawkesbury. Gallagher, using a Montreal address, checked into the Viking Motel in Port Hastings. He insisted on the room next to or above or below the union representative in the area for the organizing campaign, say motel employees. In 1971 the union had an organizing campaign going in nearby Point Tupper at the new Gulf Oil refinery. Gallagher stayed around, keeping the room next to the O.C.A.W. official. The maid could not get into the room, according to motel employees. One day in July local R.C.M.P. agents, acting on a tip from the motel's manager, put Gallagher under surveillance. The R.C.M.P. told O.C.A.W. officials that Gallagher was "bugging" the union room but that the police couldn't do anything about it since they believed, as most policemen do, that electronic eavesdropping breaks no law.

Gallagher was confronted the next day near the motel by two union officials. One, Cliff Basken, recalls, "We just tongue-lashed him". Gallagher denied that he had electronic equipment in his room, although a motel employee had entered the room and reported that he had seen the devices, including a tape recorder and an amplifier. The electric socket on the baseboard of one wall had been removed, giving a microphone a virtual tunnel into the union room next door.

A few days before the confrontation between Gallagher and the union staff men in Port Hastings, negotiations reached a critical stage in Toronto at the Royal York Hotel with the oil industry's leader, Gulf, and the O.C.A.W. Canadian director Neil Reimer was at the hotel, having flown in from his office in Edmonton, Alberta, for the final stage of the bargaining. A man whose description fits Brian Gallagher and who registered under the name "Gage" asked for the room next to Reimer's. When a desk clerk commented to Reimer, "Your friend Mr. Gage is already here," Reimer asked to be moved to a different room. "Gage" moved with him. The "Do Not Disturb" sign was on the door next to Reimer's constantly while negotiations continued. Hotel maids were not allowed to enter. After "Gage" checked out, before dawn, Reimer got into the 12th-floor room, 12-265. He found that someone had tampered with the baseboard socket on the common wall with his room. He found a receipt from a Toronto stereo equipment store for recording tapes. The hotel management has refused to discuss the incident.

"Gage" is a popular pseudonym in the labour spy racket. In the 1969 Teamsters' strike at Lakehead Freightways in Port Arthur and Fort William, Ontario, a man registered as "Gage" insisted on a room touching the temporary headquarters of a Teamsters' negotiator. "Gage" got the room below, No. 612, according to the Teamster official. The Teamster negotiator presumes he was "bugged".

In June of 1972 Reimer of the Oil, Chemical and Atomic Workers was back in Toronto at the Royal York for a national conference of his union. A private investigator detected an electronic transmitter hidden somewhere in Reimer's room with the use of an R.F. Detector, a device that picks up signals from concealed eavesdropping equipment.

Gallagher's 1972 activity appeared to centre on the construction industry. He apparently is anxious to build up his contacts in the building-trades unions.

The widespread sales of electronic listening devices have reduced somewhat the need for labour spies who infiltrate unions and send their copious handwritten reports to post office boxes. The new spy is small enough to conceal in your hand and powerful enough to broadcast a conversation for blocks. How many wiretaps are on the telephones of union offices, and how many listening devices are concealed in union offices and workers' locker-rooms, cannot be estimated. Many officials in the labour movement presume that their telephones have been tapped. Some confidential discussions are conducted between officials speaking from pay telephones.

Wiretapping, intercepting telephone messages, is an old practice among practitioners of anti-union espionage. One U.S. agency, the National Corporation Service, was providing wiretapping for management clients as early as the 1930's. The presence of the "bug" is pervasive in society. Using electronic eavesdropping equipment against unions is one of countless ways in which the privacy of ordinary citizens has been penetrated. Whatever the public may think of the practice of electronic eavesdropping or wiretapping, governments have been slow to move, probably because politicians and many of their constituents believe that eavesdropping is only used against those who have done something "wrong". How many would disagree with the idea that "if you haven't done anything wrong you have nothing to hide"?

But people with nothing to hide don't realize that what they keep to themselves, no matter how innocent, may be of value to someone else.

It is obvious that anyone who has ever applied for a loan, asked for a divorce, filed an insurance claim for injury or damage, worked in a competitive "name-brand" business or major industry, or been a witness to a case that landed in court could be under the surveillance of electronic eavesdropping. A public inquiry commission set up by the British Columbia government reported in 1967 that electronic "bugging" was commonplace in car dealerships, health "spas" and dance-lesson studios.[22] Executives of 10 car dealers testified, and the commission concluded that "all made use of . . . listening devices".[23] The businessmen engaged in this surreptitious listening all claimed it was to help improve the pitch of their salesmen, or in the case of the gyms and dance studios, to weed out "perverts".

The B.C. privacy commission heard testimony from several private investigators and police officials on the availability of electronic snooping devices. The electronic ears and eyes "appear to be readily available to anyone who can pay for them," the commission stated.[24]

The B.C. probe found that sometimes spies using electronic ears were spying on each other. "Apparently bugging of stock brokers' offices is quite a business in the city of Vancouver," the B.C. commission reported.[25]

One popular justification for permitting free citizens living in a democracy to be spied on with electronic listening devices is that "the police do it". The Protection of Privacy Act introduced in 1971 by federal Justice Minister John Turner (and slowly creeping towards enactment in the middle of 1972) institutionalizes the invasion of privacy, giving legal blessing to the practice of the state peeping furtively into the secrets of its people. The bill would outlaw private wiretapping and other kinds of electronic surveillance and provide up to five-year prison terms for violators. It would permit the police to tap telephones and use other "bugs" to gather information on a wide range of suspected criminal activities with the permission of a judge, a provincial attorney-general or the federal solicitor-general.

To those who already suspect their telephones are bugged for union activity, the Turner bill is of little comfort. The police have wiretapped aggressively. The Liberal government's bill to restrict electronic eavesdropping will still allow politicians to be judge and jury over whose telephone is tapped. The temptation to turn routine police investigations into dragnets for political purposes will be great. Resting authorization in the judiciary makes a convincing argument, although the courts historically have tended to buttress the police establishment, the corporate power centres and the government in power.

The police establishment resents any suggestion that police abuse their spy privileges or that electronic eavesdropping is too routine, too extensive. Critics are accused of disloyalty. The chief of police of Vancouver, testifying at the British Columbia commission into the invasion of privacy, stated the police attitude succinctly, when he told his critics their opposition "is nothing more than an expression of non-confidence in the integrity of the policing profession today. Let the record speak for itself, and those who feel so inclined will be found wanting for evidence to support this opinion."[26]

Although evidence is scarce that the police have arbitrarily or whimsically tapped citizens' telephones (and the police know it's scarce), evidence does exist that some police and governments have been cavalier about the privacy of their taxpayers. In the United States, President Lyndon B. Johnson ordered all wiretapping to cease unless it had the approval of the attorney-general. Johnson's attorney-general, Ramsey Clark, turned down repeated requests from J. Edgar Hoover, the head of the Federal Bureau of Investigation, to tap the phones of Dr. Martin Luther King Jr.—up to two days before King was slain in Memphis, Tennessee, in 1968. But the F.B.I. went ahead anyway and eavesdropped on the conversations of the renowned civil-rights fighter.[27]

Under the amendments to the Criminal Code brought in by the Liberal government in 1971, the federal Justice Department would be able to authorize wiretapping in cases of "national security", precisely the justification used by the F.B.I. to monitor Dr. King.

The case of ex-Premier Drew's "Ontario Gestapo" (see earlier in this chapter) is a vivid Canadian example of how willing politicians can be to abuse the civil rights of opponents. By default the Liberal government's wiretapping legislation sanctions untoward eavesdropping into the lives of innocent people.

The police are eager to wiretap. Between 1968 and late 1971 the number of wiretaps authorized by the chief of police in Toronto quadrupled. In the first 11 months of 1971 the chief authorized 203 wiretaps.[28] The police decline to say how long their taps remain in place. Suppose three months is the average. The average Canadian telephone handles 1,630 calls a year, or about 406 calls in three months.[29] Based on the number of lines monitored by the Toronto police, the police could have listened in on more than 82,000 conversations in 1971. Obviously the police establishment's alibi and rationalization for wiretapping—that only suspected unlawful activity is being spied on—fails the test of logic. In 82,000 conversations, how many discussed criminal activity? What else did the police overhear? And who now has the information they overheard?

How much extraneous information is sucked up in a routine police (or other) wiretap for suspected criminal activity is demonstrated by the disclosures in a recent U.S. Supreme Court case. While tapping just one telephone, police officers in New York City recorded conversations involving at the other end of the line the Julliard School of Music, the Brooklyn Law School, the offices of Western Union, a bank, several restaurants, a real estate company, a drug store, many attorneys, an importer, a dry cleaning store, a number of taverns, a garage and the Prudential Insurance Company.[30]

Former U.S. Attorney-General Ramsey Clark has become a vigorous opponent of wiretapping by anybody. Clark calls the practice not only unimportant in crime fighting (the police administration's most common excuse) but detrimental to efficient police work. It takes two to six men to operate a tap, Clark says, and it could take months, "even years" to get something juicy enough from the eavesdrop to begin a prosecution.[31]

Wiretapping is much touted as a crucial police tool against organized crime, but Clark disputes its value. Not a single conviction resulted from information gathered through wiretapping from the late 1950's until 1965, Clark says.[32]

The Canadian Civil Liberties Association opposes the Liberal government's bill as being too broad in the scope of crimes it includes for wiretap authorization. "Surreptitious snooping is no less an invasion of privacy when it is committed by a police officer with a lofty motive than when it is committed by a private citizen with a selfish motive," says the general counsel of the association, A. Alan Borovoy.

Even as a crime-busting tool, wiretapping is too extreme an invasion of the right to be left alone—even if it worked. A noted American jurist, William O. Douglas, once said the following about the attempts by police and government to sanctify wiretapping by saying it's a crime-fighting apparatus:

The use of torture is also effective in getting confessions from suspects. But a civilized society does not sanction it. . . .

The free state offers what a police state denies—the privacy of the home, the dignity and peace of mind of the individual. That precious right to be left alone is violated once the police enter our conversations.[33]

"Privacy is central to dignity and liberty," comments the Canadian Civil Liberties Association. "The human being in our society requires a retreat from public view, even when 'objectively' he has nothing to hide. He needs a secluded sector in which to ventilate his hopes and fears, his loves and hates."

Invasion of privacy, as one lawyer puts it, "is something that cannot be undone". The labour movement, given the record of the government, the courts and the police in the organization of workers, has a great deal to fear from wiretapping, even eavesdropping conducted ostensibly only by the police, only for suspected criminal activity. The scope of the Liberal government's bill is wide; almost any form of political or social dissent could be prey to wiretapping. If dissenters, as union sympathizers are to a large degree, fear their words will be monitored, they will impose self-censorship, and fear will serve the purposes of labour's traditional enemies.

In such an atmosphere, the freedom of speech guaranteed in the Bill of Rights is meaningless since it is no freedom at all if people are afraid to use it.

Like labour spying, electronic eavesdropping is a mind-probe to find out what people think. Under the custody of the police, the danger is less, but only slightly so, if wholesale electronic prying is reduced but not erased. Organized labour cannot consider itself safe. As the Canadian Civil Liberties Association puts it, "Recent experience has taught us that many police officers have an unlimited capacity to apprehend danger."

Faith that the police will protect the privacy of citizens doing nothing wrong was not enhanced by the conviction of a Metro constable with Richard Grange in the Redpath Sugars wiretap case. To the Redpath strikers, the police put themselves under more suspicion the night that the union stakeout trapped Barry Chapman with a tape recorder (allegedly bought by Richard Grange) in his hands. The union members who had trapped the policeman behind their strike headquarters found themselves being questioned in the police station for almost an hour while their lawyer, Clayton Ruby, was kept outside. When Ruby called the deputy chief of police, John Ackroyd, to complain, Ruby told the trial, Ackroyd "didn't know" whether it was an authorized police wiretap.

142

The further cause for doubt that wiretap legislation will curtail anti-labour espionage is that enforcement of the new Criminal Code amendments will be left to the same governments, judicial system and police forces who have served as timeless foes of working-class people's organizations. The public could reasonably doubt the determination of the police and government to enforce wiretap legislation. In the United States, for instance, private wiretapping and surveillance has been illegal since 1968. But the department of one state government that regulates detective agencies has been quoted as saying it believes half its licenced private investigators are breaking the law.[34]

Without laws specifically prohibiting anti-union espionage and strikebreaking, there can be no assurance that worker organizations will thrive in this country. The enemies of labour who protect their prerogatives so jealously believe themselves above the law. So bold were labour spies in the United States that one Pinkerton man even "shadowed" an assistant secretary of labour, Edward F. McGrady, while he worked as a conciliator in a 1935 General Motors strike in Ohio and Michigan.[35] In Detroit the spy listened at the labour department official's hotel-room wall, but the investigator testified at the La Follette hearings that he heard nothing because the labour department man "mumbled".[36]

That would remain an obscure vignette from a past long gone except that a similar mystery involving a government official occurred in 1971 in Nova Scotia. The official was a mediator with the Nova Scotia Department of Labour. At a hotel in Amherst he found a wireless transmitter in a room he had rented for negotiating meetings. "I have nothing definite to link it to the company," the Labour Department man says. He took the "bug" to his superiors in the Labour Department, but nothing was done about it. Eavesdropping, he says, could upset the entire foundation of the government's intervention in management-labour disputes. His own job, he says, "would become impossible".

"The essence of third-party mediation is confidentiality, and it must be preserved," says the Labour Department troubleshooter. He presumes the device was used to tape-record conversations. He is afraid spying on the bargaining process could subvert collective bargaining "if the tape got into the wrong hands or some guy used it unscrupulously".

The wireless transmitters available today in Canada are activated by the sound of human voices. They amplify the noises, which are picked up by the spy with a simple FM-band radio receiver or recorded by a concealed tape recorder. One wireless transmitter obtained from a Canadian Driver Pool strikebreaker is so small that it stunned a Toronto supplier of electronic eavesdropping devices when he was shown it. He remarked that not even the Toronto police have anything as sophisticated.

Testimony at the trial of Richard Grange and the Toronto policeman charged with him in October, 1971, revealed how useful the array of snooping devices on the market can be to professional strikebreakers—and how extensively they are used. The owner of a suburban Toronto radio store called Stereo City Limited, Robert Soviak, admitted selling tape recorders, cassettes of blank recording tapes and "around a dozen" wireless microphones to Grange.[37] A former strikebreaker, Gregory Ross, recalled that he had listened to a tape recording with Grange and another employee of Grange's Canadian Driver Pool, Brian Bertram. Ross testified that Bertram said the tape had been made at Kenroc Tools Limited, which used Grange's services. It contained the voices of striking Kenroc employees.[38] After listening to another tape, Ross recalled, Grange remarked to him "that this would keep the operations of Canadian Driver Pool one step ahead of the union".[39]

It is ironic that Grange and the policeman, Barry Chapman, were charged for the wiretap on the strike headquarters of the International Chemical Workers' Union with "conspiracy . . . to effect an unlawful purpose". The almost ancient allegation of criminal conspiracy used so often against unions turned out to be the charge that convicted a strikebreaker. The "unlawful purpose" was divulging "the purport or the substance of the conversation or messages to any one or more of their own number, their agents or other unknown persons not being lawfully authorized or directed to do so". The sentences, $500 fines against both, and the convictions, were appealed a few weeks after Judge Garth Moore judged the two men guilty on March 28, 1972. The two alleged conspirators chose a trial with no jury and did not take the stand in their own defence.

Judge Moore ruled that although there was no specific law against wiretapping, a conspiracy could be found in the common law, not written statutes, to cover "wrongful acts". Quoting a legal precedent, Moore said, "There can be no doubt that all confederacies whatsoever, wrongfully to prejudice a third person are highly criminal at common law. . . ."[40]

Moore concluded, "The purpose of this conspiracy was to carry out 20th-century eavesdropping and divulge the result.

This activity, in my opinion, would surely work to the injury of the union in this case. . . ."[41]

Lawyer David Humphrey, representing constable Chapman, had argued that even if the prosecution could prove there had been wiretapping and that it involved his client, the purpose was not unlawful, but honourable: to avoid picket-line confrontations. Considering the amount of violence in strikes, Humphrey asserted, the police "should take the wiretaps off prostitutes' lines and do something about violence".

The detectives who charged Grange and Chapman also found the remains of what they stated was definitely a wiretap at another strike where Driver Pool worked, at Kimberly-Clark Canada Limited in St. Catharines. A piece of wire found behind the strike headquarters of United Auto Workers Local 1566 in Galt, Ontario, matches the grey cord attached to the tape recorder found in the alley behind the Redpath Sugars' strike headquarters. The U.A.W. had struck Wean United, a manufacturer of machinery, in February, 1972, and the company retained Driver Pool's front organization, Canadian Specialized Security Limited. A battery, an obscure brand, was also found behind the U.A.W. headquarters. The same kind of batteries were used to power one of the tape recorders confiscated in the Redpath wiretapping.

At another company that used Driver Pool's services, Union Carbide Canada Limited in Oakville, Ontario, the microphone for a tape recorder was found hidden in an air duct in the employees' locker room in April 1972, just before a strike began. The tape recorder was found nearby and turned over to the Oakville police department, which says it investigated but didn't charge anyone.

Notes

1. Horan, James D., *The Pinkertons: The Detective Dynasty That Made History*, Crown Publishers, Inc., New York, N.Y., 1967, p. 508.
2. Cited in Taylor and Witney, *op. cit.*, p. 120.
3. Horan, *op. cit.*, p. 509.
4. Amidon, *op. cit.*, p. 306.
5. Huberman, Leo, *The Labour Spy Racket*, Modern Age Books, Inc., New York, N.Y., 1937, p. 6.
6. Amidon, *op. cit.*, p. 266.
7. *Ibid.*
8. Jamieson, *op cit.*, p. 47.
9. Cited in Huberman, *op. cit.*, p. 33.

10. Huberman, *op. cit.*, p. 21.
11. Caplan, Gerald L., "The Ontario 'Gestapo' Affair, 1943-1945," *Canadian Journal of Economics and Political Science*, August, 1964, pp. 343-359.
12. Caplan, Gerald L., "The Failure of Canadian Socialism: The Ontario Experience, 1932-1945," *The Canadian Journal of Economics and Political Science*, June, 1963, pp. 116-117.
13. Jamieson, *op. cit.*, p. 58.
14. *Toronto Star*, January 15, 1972.
15. "Mr. Willkie Pleads Guilty," *The New Republic*, September 16, 1940, p. 373.
16. "The Labour Spy," *The New Republic*, January 5, 1938, p. 241.
17. Caplan, "The Ontario 'Gestapo' Affair, 1943-1945," *op. cit.*, p. 355.
18. Huberman, *op. cit.*, p. 74.
19. *Ibid.*, p. 6.
20. *Labour Organizations in Canada*, Economics and Research Branch, Canada Department of Labour, Queen's Printer, Ottawa, 1970 edition, p. XV.
21. "Mr. Willkie Pleads Guilty," *op. cit.*, p. 373.
22. Sargent R. A., *Report of the Commission of Inquiry into Invasion of Privacy*, Vancouver, British Columbia, 1967, pp. 11-24.
23. *Ibid.*, p. 18.
24. *Ibid.*, p. 34.
25. *Ibid.*, p. 36. The B.C. commission was established to investigate the bugging of a union official's hotel room. Lloyd Craig, the president of the Pulp and Paper Workers of Canada, was found dead in his room at the Ritz Hotel in Vancouver, November 5, 1966. Craig had led a breakaway to form new his union from members of the International Brotherhood of Pulp, Sulphite and Paper Mill Workers. An investigation into his death, apparently of natural causes, disclosed that the international union had contacted the R.C.M.P. about the alleged disappearance of $40,000 from the union and the future plans of the new rival union. A Mountie advised E. P. O'Neal, an organizer for the international, to contact a private investigator named Bud Graham, who admitted in the subsequent probe that he monitored and tape recorded conversations in Craig's hotel room from an adjoining room. The Canadian director of the international union, L. H. Lorrain, told the commission that O'Neal's decision to retain an investigator and permit electronic eavesdropping was not sanctioned or condoned by the union. The commissioner concluded that O'Neal could not be found "blame-worthy when one considers all the circumstances".
26. *Ibid.*, p. 49.
27. Schlossberg, Stephen I., and Whitman, M. Jay, *Brief of the International Union, United Automobile, Aerospace and Agricultural Implement Workers of America (UAW) as Amicus Curiae in Support of Respondents, United States of America v. United States District Court for the Eastern District of Michigan, Southern Division and Honorable Damon J. Keith*, October term, 1971, pp. 34-35.
28. *The Globe and Mail*, December 23, 1971.
29. *Telephone Statistics, 1970*, Statistics Canada, Information Canada, Ottawa, March, 1972, p. 14.
30. Letter from the Canadian Civil Liberties Association to Justice Minister John Turner, January 26, 1972.

31. Berkley, *op. cit.*, pp. 194-195.
32. C.C.L.A. letter, *op. cit.*
33. Cited in Schlossberg and Whitman, *op. cit.*, p. 12.
34. Kakalik, James S., and Wildhorn, Sorrel, *The Law and Private Police, Prepared for the Department of Justice*, The Rand Corporation, Santa Monica, California, 1971, Volume IV, p. 33.
35. Amidon, *op. cit.*, p. 265.
36. "The Pinkertons Testify," *op. cit.*, p. 227.
37. Trial transcript, *op. cit.*, p. 319.
38. *Ibid.*, p. 275.
39. *Ibid.*, p. 256.
40. *Ibid.*, p. 495.
41. *Ibid.*, p. 497.

8

The Fear Merchants

I sit on a man's back, choking him and making him carry me,
and yet assure myself and others that I am very sorry for
him and wish to lighten his load by all possible means—
except by getting off his back.

Leo Tolstoy

In a current movie, *The Garden of the Finzi-Continis*, protag-
onists discuss the retrenchment of rights of the Jewish minority
during the rise of fascism in Italy. One diminishes the ghettoiza-
tion of the Jews. But the other is more apprehensive and comments, "There are few enough rights for anyone." The comment is profound, because human rights are seldom cherished
until they are restricted.

The uninhibited surveillance of union members who are exer-
cising freedoms under labour laws and the Bill of Rights is a
threat to everyone's civil liberties. It is passé to observe that behind every spy is a tyrant. Yet Canadian governments and businessmen have condoned police-state tactics like spying and professional strikebreaking by freelance goons and dangerous criminals, in the naive supposition that, as long as these industrial
mercenaries direct their plots against the unions, the two-thirds
of the population who are not in unions are perfectly safe. But
like the Mafia, the agents of labour espionage and unionbusting
are the ones who make the rules. Among the Mafia, it is said
that newspaper reporters and policemen are not to be killed. But
suppose the rules change? The government of Ontario has let
private armies open civil wars on union men and union women,
but no one can be sure that the war will be contained.

Spying and strikebreaking create fear. And fear is big business
in this country. Workers in any profession, business, office or
factory, cannot be sure any more that their every move is not
watched, photographed, monitored, tape-recorded, transcribed,

reported and filed away. Anti-labour spy rings and credit checking firms have uncountable files on the life histories, work records and private lives of ordinary citizens who have done no more than punch a time clock, take out a union membership, attend a meeting or sign a petition. Retail credit agencies alone have over half a million confidential reports for managements' eyes only.[1] This intelligence can be tape recorded, put on computer tapes, packaged and concealed so tightly that the records of thousands of individual Canadians can be taken across the border to the United States in a suitcase. Some could join the more than 3,000,000 other files in the headquarters of the Wackenhut Corporation, an American private police force.

Wackenhut is the latest of the U.S. police businesses to penetrate a lucrative Canadian market in fear. In 1971 Wackenhut took over three Canadian private investigation and security-guard forces, the largest being the Toronto-based firm owned by Raymond Anning, today president of Wackenhut of Canada Limited. The police-business takeover was accomplished with little publicity and no apparent concern by the government of Ontario for the privacy or protection of its population. George Ben, a Liberal party member of the Legislature, questioned Conservative government ministers about the takeover in August. "The possibility of the growth of private armies . . . is enough to give all thinking politicians concern," Ben said.[2] (Two months later he was defeated in the provincial election.)

The other U.S. investigation agencies operating in Canada also keep files from their operatives' reports. Pinkerton's had more than 1,500,000 files in 1961.[3] The William J. Burns International Detective Agency ostensibly has a much smaller dossier room, with 140,000 files in 1959, but claims these are all on criminals.[4]

The Wackenhut takeover is the most controversial because it directly links an ambitious and aggressive professional strike-breaking company with the archetypal private policeman, George R. Wackenhut, whose personality and methods have alarmed American authorities for some time. Wackenhut himself, a former F.B.I. physical-education instructor, is depicted commonly by American authorities as "a militant foe of organized labour"[5] who proselytizes for the right-wing John Birch Society. (Shortly after Wackenhut invaded Canada, curiously enough, so did the Birchers, claiming Prime Minister Trudeau was a tool of an international communist conspiracy.) Wackenhut's guard work, investigating and substantial contracts with various federal and state government agencies in the U.S. have made the corporation the third biggest of its kind in the world, with $48.5 million in annual revenues, about one-third of Pinkerton's revenue and one-half of Burns'.* Wackenhut also has Ontario government contracts. One is to supply guards at courtrooms. The company sells and leases electric alarm systems, too, and is even in the publishing business, distributing free monthly issues of the *Wackenhut Security Review*. Predictably, the Wackenhut house organ details various schemes by communists to subvert the world's young people. The *Review* has a circulation of more than 60,000. Wackenhut calls communism "the most vicious form of organized crime ever perpetrated on the human race".[6] Fighting real organized crime is not as easy as paper wars with communist conspiracies, as Wackenhut found out when the Republican governor of Florida hired him in 1967 to fight the Mafia. Wackenhut's impact appears to have been minimal. A one-time reporter who specialized in organized crime writing for the *Miami Herald* joined the Wackenhut army but quit soon afterwards. "A hoax is being perpetrated on the people of Florida, and I will not be part of that hoax," he said.[7] Wackenhut obviously knew something about crime fighting, though. In 1955 he was cited for contempt by a Florida court for intimidating a witness.[8] During the time when Wackenhut was employed by former Florida Governor Claude Kirk there were complaints that a Wackenhut agent had unlawfully searched a "suspect's" home.

George Russell Wackenhut is a man who markets fear. He even has a yacht named *Security Risk*. Though Wackenhut claims he is not a John Birch Society member himself, the Wackenhut Corporation board of directors looks like an abbreviated list for a George Wallace testimonial dinner. One director, Ralph E. Davis, is a member of the national council of the Birch Society. Davis runs Wackenhut's U.S. west coast operations.[9] Another director is Loyd Wright, who praised the Birch Society in an unsuccessful campaign for the U.S. Senate a few years ago. He is also the "national strategy committee" of a far-right Pentagon-booster lobby called the American Security Council. Another director is retired General Mark W. Clark, also of the American Security Council. Another is retired Captain Eddie Rickenbacker, one of the foremost right-wing spokes-

*Source: Kakalik, James S., and Wildhorn, Sorrel, *Private Police in the United States: Findings and Recommendations, Prepared for the Department of Justice*, The Rand Corporation, Santa Monica, California, Volume 1, December, 1971, p. 14.

men in the U.S. and a campaigner against income taxes and the United Nations.[10]

Wackenhut's man in the Canadian end of the operation is Raymond Anning, who says, "Our having been acquired in no way jeopardizes the operations of Canadian business."[11] Wackenhut's Canadian business includes professional strikebreaking and industrial espionage. Boldly, almost defiantly, Anning has huckstered his specialty with indelicate advertising and promotion (see Chapter 5). The spice in the salesmanship is paranoia. In one brochure Anning offers "Intelligence reports before union negotiations. (What is really going on? What does the union really want?)" Half of Anning's staff of nearly 50 investigators work undercover posing as employees, Anning told an interviewer in 1969. "Intelligence reports during negotiations" are offered Wackenhut management-clients.[12]

The multi-million-dollar revenues collected by the spy businesses indicate how much management is willing to pay to know everything about its employees. A former Wackenhut investigator says that Ray Anning told him just one spy account is worth $50,000 a year. Some employers who have used Wackenhut complain that they need spies to see why employee morale is low. They fear bad labour-management rapport leads to thefts—or unions. A former Canadian Wackenhut spy in a major retail food chain says one reason labour-management relations were so poor was Wackenhut: the employees felt management was spying on them.

Labour spies who infiltrate unions are usually put on the payroll of the company who hires them, to avoid suspicion. Since spies, like strikebreakers, are usually paid more than the regular workers, Wackenhut pays the difference between the going spy salary ($3.50 to $4 an hour) and the lower-paying union rate. In "closed shops", where the union has contract protection against free-loaders and new employees must pay union dues, check-offs also are paid by the spy agency or the company that hires the spies.

Despite the availability of sophisticated electronic snooping devices, human spying remains as popular as ever in Canadian business. A human spy can get set down on paper emotions, unspoken actions and other observations that no electric gizmo can.

A former Canadian Wackenhut spy who infiltrated employees who belong to a Teamster local says his own effectiveness was much like a wiretap. He was a human dragnet, sopping up everything he could see and learn. He was told that he was planted in the company's shop to look for the source of restiveness among members of the union. But like most spies, he learned a great deal more about the employees he followed. "I could have reported who their girl friends were and who was taking dope, all sorts of things. I could have ruined their future." This spy says he was honest, though, and grew sick of his own work. "It's the kind of work," he reflects, "if you have any kind of conscience at all you get out of." He says his fellow professional spies "were just like snakes—cold blooded". He reported "maybe 10 per cent" of what he saw and heard by spying on his "fellow employees". But he says that if he were less scrupulous, he could have compromised some employees and could even have done a "shake-down" for his own profit.

Such a business naturally is the stepchild of the professional strikebreaking business, and historically has been so. The La Follette committee in the United States reported as long ago as 1939 that "spies precede strikes; strikeguards and strikebreakers accompany them. The connection between the two forms of service is convenient for the employer who wishes to destroy a union, and therefore lucrative for the agency that supplies them."[13]

Such a lucrative business would naturally attract Richard Grange and his Canadian Driver Pool. The strikebreakers after the strike has begun are usually the same people who were spies before the strike. Ex-Grange spies say that some of the companies that have put Driver Pool spies on the payroll include Elias Rogers, Gidon Industries Limited, Central Precision Limited, and Kamro Lighting Products.

Driver Pool spies in Kamro, a Toronto company organized by the United Steelworkers of America, included Vince Gorman and Bill Hollingshead, two veteran strikebreakers. (The union managed to get a first contract without a strike, a rarity in an industrial ghetto plant in Ontario.) A Grange spy at Elias Rogers, an oil-burner concern, says he attended union meetings prior to bargaining and during negotiations and met twice a week with Grange and a company official to discuss his findings. "I told the company what the men would accept," says the spy. "You listen to little groups of guys that pop up after a union meeting and so forth—you get it."

To many, no doubt, it sounds astounding that a company would pay twice and three times the "union rate" for spies rather than listen to a union negotiating committee elected by the company's workers. But in union espionage, the medium, the spy system, can be as important as the message from the spies.

Observers were astonished in the United States when the industrial espionage system was exposed in the late 1930's. Wrote one commentator, "There is nothing in the report of a labour spy which an employer could not learn from a frank and aboveboard discussion with representatives of his employees. The continued use of paid informers is a tribute to the effective sales talk of the agencies, but a large question mark on both the intelligence and the social ideals of those who employ them."[14]

Regardless of the information the spy system feeds management, its very existence is anti-union. Even if not a useful particle of information is provided, the tension and the distrust that the spy system creates are effective anti-union weapons. It is not necessary for the labour spy actually to get secret information for the employer to prevent organization of the employer's workers. If they think they are spied upon, contact among employees is more guarded. Organizing is tougher. Union leaders become suspects. Divisiveness results. The "plant", without ever writing a report or tattling to the management, can poison effective organizing.

The legality of the hundreds of operatives recruited by professional strikebreaking companies, security services, management "consultants" and "industrial engineers" is questionable. Are these spies not really unlicenced private investigators? Clearly some of their activities are more than questionable. Organizers for the International Union of District 50 remember an organizing campaign cut off at a Toronto company, Federal Equipment (Fedquip Limited now), when a labour spy brought a case of beer into the plant and got more than a dozen union supporters drinking on company time. They were fired. With the key union supporters dismissed, the union lost a vote for bargaining rights.

Other spies specialize in setting up management-controlled company unions. The company-union spies discourage workers from joining real unions with higher dues and encourage localized, ineffective and inexpensive associations. The company unions go by a variety of names. "Employee representation plan" is a common company-union front phrase. In the past 10 years, says the Canadian director of the Oil, Chemical and Atomic Workers' International Union, Neil Reimer, the same three spies helped set up company unions in two oil refineries, a fertilizer operation and a chemical factory in British Columbia and Alberta. "These types are always the first to be hired when a plant opens," says Reimer. He says at least one spy in the company-union business admitted to O.C.A.W. officials that he had received extra inducements from a company to keep out real unions.

The information from private investigators and union spies can be used to compromise employees. Words like blackmail and extortion are not too strong to describe the results. Reimer remembers an organizing drive in the oil industry that was sabotaged when a company executive called a leader of the campaign with a direct threat. The organizer's brother had once been in the Communist Party of Canada. The executive indicated that the organizer's brother would lose his job if his boss learned about his background. Reimer recalls another organizer who gave up his union work when a management man told him, "We know you're having an affair with a woman—do you want your wife to know?"

Inside the typical office or factory, a different world exists, with its own set of values, different from the values of society as a whole. Procedures and disciplinary measures that would be considered fascistic if used on the sidewalk outside are tolerated as the exercise of management rights.

The polygraph (lie detector) has become fashionable in North American industry. Employees have been submitted to searches of their lockers, cars, purses, toolkits and lunchboxes as corporations defend their right to know as much as they want about workers' lives. Employees have been watched in washrooms and offices. Their conversations have been recorded without their knowledge.

"Anyone representing employees soon becomes painfully aware of an increasingly rapid erosion of their personal rights," says one labour lawyer. Unions and individuals who protest such arbitrary management spying, he says, run into the widespread code of corporate life that "the majority who do as they are told are always right and that the dissenter is probably wrong".[15]

The government as an employer is no better. Statistics Canada (the former Dominion Bureau of Statistics) said in 1971, for example, that it was considering photographing and fingerprinting its 4,000 employees.[16] Cartage companies and other concerns using delivery trucks have installed devices called tachographs, "mechanical spies", in the words of one labour arbitrator, which register engine speeds and idling time.

The United Auto Workers protested in 1971 when Ford Motor Company of Canada Limited installed closed circuit television at gates to the company's Oakville, Ontario, plant. Employees, instead of passing a human guard, now approach the gates, speak to the cameras and are allowed to enter by a guard monitoring the TV screens. Fearing the company would soon install the cameras inside the plant, the union filed a grievance. The arbitrator upheld the company. "The mere fact that certain procedures may be embarrassing and distasteful does not mean that they are contrary to the collective agreement. . . ." said the arbitrator, J. F. W. Weatherill.

Rarely has a company's "right" to spy electronically or otherwise on its workers been challenged successfully. The corporation's right to use human spies remains restricted only by the company's ability or inability to get away with it. Some states in the U.S. have outlawed the practice outright or made it virtually impossible for labour spies to function, by requiring that spy agencies register the names of all their operatives. The list is a public record. In one exceptional American case, an arbitrator ruled that an employer broke his contract's provision guaranteeing "beneficial working conditions" by installing closed-circuit television to spy on workers. In that case the arbitrator ruled that the television spy "imposes an appreciable and intolerable burden on them (the workers)". Far from providing the incentive not to goof off, cameras have "an inhibiting effect as to prevent employees from performing their work with confidence and ease". The arbitrator called the cameras "an affront to the dignity of man".[17]

Major corporations, influenced by the security hysteria, are stringing their plants and offices with electronic surveillance equipment. Some have recruited big security forces, including plainclothes plant detectives. Usually, stringent "security" measures are instituted without the approval or consultation of unions. The practice creates suspicion that the company has enlisted an army of anti-union spies along with its routine plant guards. Agents of a corporation army do not have to be licenced as security guards or private investigators. Only contract guards and spies are covered by provincial security-licence legislation. But corporate police work is a grey area that may go beyond the law. The companies that recruit these police forces obviously believe they have more power than the law.

They don't think that workers who spend one-third of their lives in shops or plants or offices should have the same civil rights on the job that they expect under the Bill of Rights in their home or on the street. Their right "to life, liberty, security of the person and enjoyment of property", as the Bill of Rights says, ends in private enterprise when that right collides with management prerogatives.

The danger of a corporate mercenary to the free association of workers is the same as the threat from private contract police who drive trucks over union picket lines, intimidate and rough up strikers and post themselves as strikeguards. The civil rights of our entire society are at stake. As the La Follette committee reported to the people of the United States after years of probing anti-labour rackets:

No pretense of protecting the State against supposed dangers, or of preserving "law and order," or blatant assertion of a private economic interest can justify private usurpation of State authority.[18]

There can be no doubt that corporate police forces are becoming bigger and more aggressive. At Douglas Aircraft Company of Canada Limited near Toronto, plainclothes investigators who are the manufacturer's own employees (but not licenced as investigators off the company premises) have tailed employees to meetings. They have visited workers at their homes, interrogated landlords and neighbours of employees and used an informant on a charter flight to the British Isles. All this shadowing was done under the euphemism of "security" and allegedly to check up on whether absent employees really were sick or disabled. In the process the company has created a sizeable intelligence force that could turn its skills against the unions representing company employees, and may be doing so already. The chiefs of the 37-man force are all ex-military or city policemen. Their investigators have used field glasses and cameras on employees inside the plant, says Frank Fairchild, a staff representative of the United Auto Workers. A local U.A.W. white-collar leader in the plant, Ray Lomas, says one man "broke down in tears" during a grilling by the Douglas police. A female employee claims Douglas police, ostensibly checking into her absenteeism one day, began questioning neighbours about her personal life and made damaging "insinuations", says Lomas. Douglas investigators have accompanied local police on a search of an employee's home for allegedly stolen tools. The employee was acquitted on charges in court, but the company fired him anyway. The U.A.W. filed a grievance and the man got his job back. Another employee, ironically a guard, was fired after his arrest for alleged possession of drugs. He was acquitted but not reinstated. Another man was fired when Douglas police allegedly found three guns in his car, which was parked in a company lot. The man was reinstated when he explained that the guns, which weren't loaded, were part of several possessions he had piled on the back seat of his car because he was moving that day.

Business and industry are so infested with human and electronic surveillance today that many employees live a life under glass. How much of the spying and "security" is to keep employees weak and unions scarce cannot be known until the public can look into the private lives of corporations the way corporate executives look into the private lives of the public.

Notes

1. *The Globe and Mail*, March 20, 1972.
2. *The Globe and Mail*, August 28, 1971.
3. "We Never Sleep," *Newsweek*, July 31, 1961, p. 64.
4. "The Super Sleuths," *Newsweek*, August 31, 1959, p. 67.
5. "The Great Wackenhut," *The Nation*, March 6, 1967, p. 292.
6. *Ibid.*
7. Murray, Frank, "Governor Kirk's Not-So-Secret Police," *The Reporter*, March 23, 1967, p. 28.
8. *Ibid.*
9. "Spying for Industry," Ridgeway, James, *The New Republic*, May 14, 1966, p. 11.
10. Cook, Fred J., "Governor Kirk's Private Eyes," *The Nation,* May 15, 1967, p. 620.
11. Burgess, Drummond, *op. cit.*, p. 36.
12. *The* (Toronto) *Telegram*, October 28, 1969.
13. *La Follette*, Report No. 6, Part 2, Private Police Systems, p. 35.
14. Levinson, *op. cit.*, p. 729.
15. Burkey, Lee M., "Employee Surveillance: Are There Civil Rights for the Man on the Job?" *New York University 21st Annual Conference on Labour*, Proceedings), 1968, pp. 199-202.
16. *The Globe and Mail*, October 7, 1971.
17. Burkey, *op. cit.*, pp. 209-210.
18. La Follette, *op cit.*, p. 3.

Conclusion

Professional strikebreaking and anti-labour espionage are prevalent practices in Ontario. They are the elements of a conspiracy to persecute employees who form and join unions for their mutual protection and benefit.

Honest and dedicated police, judicial systems unstained by special interests and governments that make the security of their people paramount will not tolerate such arbitrary exercises in power in defiance of public policy. Union leaders and their memberships have met their obligation to society by diminishing conflict, institutionalizing it by literally removing dissent from the plants and offices of the economy into a demilitarized zone away from the work place.

Tension has been channelled from destructive action to peaceful and harmless protests and demonstrations that are protected by the Bill of Rights. On the other side of the line, there has not been as much good faith, not nearly enough respect for the rights of employees to organize without interference or intimidation.

While evangelizing for law and order and respect for property rights, managements have invited into their boardrooms criminals and hoodlums who detest the working classes and do not hesitate to trample their civil rights in pursuit of power and profits.

Union members are the shock troops in this industrial warfare. But it is obvious that spying and strikebreaking do not honour the spirit of the laws guaranteeing employees the freedom to associate and organize, to bargain and to strike when necessary.

Society, too, is harmed by the anti-union activities conducted for managements that despise and flout the liberties of their employees. No one is really safe from the industrial mercenary, the spy, the hidden microphone and the hired thug until everyone is. Professional strikebreaking is expensive to managements, and also to communities that are forced to pay for the disorder and alienation brought on by strikebreakers. What cannot be measured in dollars is the cost of these anti-union practices to the nation's people and the national conscience, the price of conditioning people to accept violence and force as legitimate weapons of social change and domestic policy.

On the basis of these findings, the government has every reason to act dramatically and swiftly, to expose the spy and strikebreaking rackets and cleanse the system. If it takes a special session of the Legislature or a public inquiry to dig out the poison, the government should have the courage to face one. Forceful laws are mandatory to clearly articulate that it is sane public policy and it is important to the welfare of the state to end anti-labour practices that corrupt the police, pervert the courts, dupe government officials and curtail the civil liberties of citizens.

No promises will accomplish industrial peace. No anguished speeches will end the bitterness gouged up by strikebreakers. Only action will matter. And there is not much time left to waste. When American authorities began exposing labour spies and organized-crime-style strikebreaking gangs, in offices across a whole continent files were set afire and records were destroyed. Investigators for the U.S. Senate Committee on Education and Labour literally plucked evidence out of wastebaskets to drive out the spies and strikebreakers. "What these companies dread more than anything else is a public inquiry," said a commentator in 1936 when the Senate began its probe. "They live in darkness and secrecy is essential for their growth."[1]

It is not enough to hope or to close one's eyes. History is blood-stained with the delusions of the smug. "Of one thing that labouring people of the world may be sure: you have dealt the Pinkerton system a death blow," said a union sympathizer after the bloody Homestead, Pennsylvania, riots when platoons of striking steelworkers fought with armed mercenaries.[2] The year was 1892.

Notes

1. "More Spies on Labour," *The New Republic*, April 22, 1936.
2. MacDonald, Dwight, *op. cit.*, p. 239.

Recommendations

The strikebreaking committee of the Ontario Federation of Labour and the Labour Council of Metropolitan Toronto, based on the findings in this report, recommended that the O.F.L. undertake the following:

1. Distribute the committee's findings as widely as possible in the labour movement.

2. Hold a one-day conference on strikebreaking to create interest in the committee's findings.

3. Establish an anti-strikebreaking task force to assist affiliated unions at their request by making available persons knowledgeable in the law, investigative procedures and communications.

4. Demand the provincial government make professional strikebreaking and anti-union espionage illegal.

5. Urge labour councils to put their local city councils on record demanding the province protect communities from professional strikebreaking and anti-labour spying.

6. Urge affiliates to negotiate "union-truck-only" clauses in contracts to curtail the growth of non-union cartage companies that supply and aid strikebreakers.

7. Publish a booklet for unionists on the rights of employees and strikers and the obligations of the police and the courts in industrial disputes.

8. Endorse mass picketing to fight strikebreaking.

9. Urge affiliated locals to circulate information on the movements and activities of professional strikebreakers.

10. Demand the provincial government close the loopholes in the Public Commercial Vehicles Act that enable unlicenced strikebreaking cartage firms to exist.

11. Campaign to make all forms of wiretapping and electronic eavesdropping illegal.

12. Persuade the Ontario Department of Labour to expand the scope of its research services to include information on unfair labour practices, working conditions and the extent of labour organization.

13. Lobby for improved relations between strikers and police by encouraging labour education programmes for police forces, by promoting citizens' review boards, by demanding upgraded police qualifications and by encouraging effective collective bargaining and organization for the police.

14. Intensify the political education committee's efforts through the New Democratic Party with the findings of the committee.

15. Contribute to the public's knowledge about unions by expanding its public relations programme and by urging the Canadian Labour Congress to study the feasibility of a mass-circulation labour periodical.

The members of the committee:

Doug Hart (Chairman),
Ralph Forsey,
Sam Fox,
Linda Hunter,
Louis Lenkinski,
Laurel MacDowell,
Terry Meagher,
Donald R. Montgomery,
Stewart Netherton,
Iona Samis,
Otto Urbanovics,
Ed Waddell.